HOLISTIC BUSINESS
LIVING IN 3D

A GUIDE TO THREE DIMENSIONAL BUSINESS
STRATEGY AND MANAGEMENT

RICHARD MOTT

Richard Mott

Holistic Business : Living in 3D

First published in Great Britain 2012 by Holistic Books

ISBN 978-0-9572440-0-9

Holistic Business

www.holisticbusiness.co

Designed by Selina Swayne

www.selinaswayne.co.uk

To Valerie, my wife, who introduced me to the work of G I Gurdjieff and without whom I might never have taken a look behind the heavy curtain of inherited bias; and to Helen, my daughter, who is wise beyond her years and keeps me straight as well as up-to-date.

Acknowledgements

I am fascinated by theory and have been inspired by many writers and speakers over the years. Edward de Bono comes in for a bit of flack but he is constantly publishing material that challenges the way we think about things. Charles Handy talks such a lot of common sense mixed in with some pretty big ideas and has certainly given me plenty to think about. Tom Peters is always worth tuning into to see what his latest thinking is (I particularly enjoyed his challenge to us to start *Thriving on Chaos* back in the nineties) and the two Norwegians Ridderstralle and Nordstrom who had such fun with their *Funky Business* and *Karaoke Capitalism*. More recently, I have been inspired by Dr Ken Robinson – first through his talks on TED and then through his book *The Element* – and his views on the impact of education and how it could be improved.

Although many of my influencers have been business writers, some of the most mind-expanding (and heart-opening) have been spiritual teachers or just observers of life and of these the greatest for me is Ram Dass or Dr Richard Alpert as he was known in the days when he was a social psychology researcher with Timothy Leary at Harvard in the mid 60's. While he has written a number of books, he comes alive when he is speaking and, luckily, many of his talks have been recorded.

My interest in spiritual matters really started when I met my wife, who was studying the work of the Georgian philosopher G I Gurdjieff. After a few years of reluctance and resistance, I decided one day to start saying "Yes" to what presented itself to me as an opportunity to do something different instead of saying, "Oh that's not for me". The result was that my life was enriched exponentially – not just my 'private' life but my business life too. One of the experiences we said "Yes" to was a trip to Egypt with Ocean WhiteHawk that included sleeping under the stars in the Sinai desert, swimming with a wild dolphin and learning the form of Tai Chi that I now teach.

In my business life I would like to recognise the contributions of Bernard Dooling, with whom I jointly founded 20·20, Malcolm

Smith, a psychologist I worked with several times and always brought more to the table than he took away, and Leslie Woodcock, who partnered me on several projects where we developed new strategic theory and practices.

In helping me to get this book out into the market I would like to say thank you to Helen Davies for her guidance during the writing process and to Tom Evans, The Bookwright, who convinced me it was time to publish. And finally, I would like to thank Selina Swayne who has designed the book wonderfully and given me inspiration and encouragement along the way.

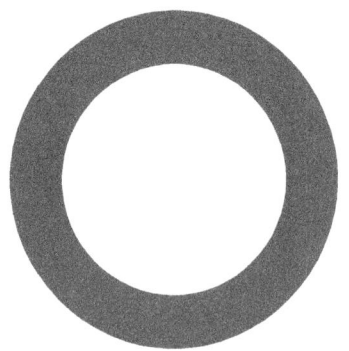

INTRODUCTION

The Need for a New Business Theory

For many years I listened to experts, read books and practised as best I could the theory of business as it stood in the late 20th century. While I enjoyed a certain degree of success, I couldn't help feeling there was more to it than I was being told about. As it turned out, I knew about the elements that were missing because I was meeting them in my life outside work – I just didn't see that they belonged in work as much as outside.

At university I studied Industrial Economics and, while it gave me a grounding in pure and applied theory, I had a strong feeling that a critical factor was missing – the human factor. Economic theory is based on macro-issues that only work if whole groups of people act in the same way driven by the same needs and desires. Without this approach, economists could not make predictions. However, I had always been interested in human psychology and this made me suspicious of any theory that ignored it.

I was taught about industrial relations and how the conflict between management and unions evolved. However, I had also worked on a building site before I went to university and I know that we were taken out on strike primarily because the local trade union representative wanted a weekend off. When learning about trading and negotiations, they never included the idea of prejudice as one of the key issues. Too many examples of the use of statistics and market research were based on single factors – which kept things simpler but not reflective of human responses.

I wanted to have a theory that took people's whims and fancies into account. Well it seems that others had the same thought and new theories of economics are being developed. The first step away from the purely rational 'science' of Economics is Behavioural Economics, which is more psychology based, and a further step is called Human Economics (or Human-Centric Economics). I look forward to further progress in this direction as I believe it will improve our chances of more accurate and useful predictions.

In 2008 the Western world experienced a lack of confidence in the financial institutions that facilitate the whole economic system. This has frightened people and in 2012 we are still not sure how the story will end. However, there could be some good news among the bad. The outcome may well lead to a new attitude towards capitalism. "It is increasingly obvious that people are motivated by morality; people are motivated by ethics," says Herbert Gintis, an emeritus professor at the University of Massachusetts and one of the leading economists studying altruism. "We may be seeing a possible renaissance of economic theory."

Business management theory, it seems to me, is very like economics in that it often ignores the human element. Industry in the UK was established during the Victorian era when managers acted like army officers, handing out instructions and demanding that particular things are done at a particular time in a particular way. This worked reasonably well as long as the workers did not have much choice and did not dare to express their opinions. However, in today's society this is no longer the case. People now can and do choose where they work and expect a great deal more job satisfaction than is the case when you are simply following orders. They will choose a company where they feel they 'fit', where they can be happy and motivated.

My breakthrough came when I understood that my view of the world as a whole (beyond the business environment) was just that – WHOLE – and that my view of business was limited to linearity, logic and learning. My view of the world as a whole had grown by exploring my feelings and my intuition. I had touched my inner knowing through practices such as meditation and Tai Chi. I had opened my mind and my heart through experiences such as seeing the sunrise on Mount Sinai and swimming with a dolphin in the Red Sea. Yet, in business, I was still relying on my traditional education to provide the answers.

If you have ever heard Dr Ken Robinson talk you will know something of what I am about to touch on – and if you haven't heard him

I strongly recommend you do so by going to the TED talks website. Dr Robinson talks about our education focusing on our bodies "from the neck up and slightly to one side" – in other words focusing on the use of the brain and, in particular, on linear thought. In fact he believes the whole educational system is linear, based on the assumption that the best thing for every child is to learn a curriculum that naturally leads to a university education, and coincidentally de-grades the arts and creativity – discouraging us from pursuing these subjects. The effect of this is to disconnect us from ourselves, to hold up the brain as the most powerful part of us and to judge anything we feel or intuit to be the object of derision. This has left us living in a one-dimensional world.

Because of the way we were all taught at school and university, there is a huge resistance to anything beyond the mental arena. Resistance is huge in all of us. We hate change and we hate new theories. During the process of writing this book, I read *Grand Design* (a book by Stephen Hawking and Leonard Mlodinow) and it struck me that the world of physics provides an interesting comparison with my own intention to introduce a new theory to the business world.

In 250 BC the Ionian scientist Aristarchus worked out that the earth moved around the sun but most of Western thought adopted Ptolemy's model from around AD 150 (based on Aristotle's philosophy) that the earth was at the centre of the cosmos and everything else moved around it. This seemed to be a logical conclusion as we couldn't feel the earth moving under our feet – how could it be moving if we didn't feel it move? It was another seventeen hundred years before this was reviewed again when in 1543 Copernicus described a world in which the sun was at rest and the planets revolved around it. All that time, partly through the dictates of the Roman Catholic Church, what we now know to be right was denied and, when Galileo advocated the Copernican model in 1633 that the earth moved around the sun, he was condemned by the church for heresy. It was another 50 years before Newton's law of gravity provided further proof and the church was forced to stand down (yet it took until 1922 before they finally acknowledged they had been wrong to condemn Galileo).

> **Analogy 1.** New theories are rarely acceptable when they contradict something we have accepted as the truth for a long time. The relevance to business leaders is that we must open our minds and refresh our understanding of the world in which we live and find new ways of being in the world. Most (but not all) organisations have already moved away from the traditional autocratic, quasi-military models of management to a more organic and motivational model. The next challenge is to take this beyond the organisation into the social and online community that will become more and more influential in the coming years – representing a quantum shift in how we run businesses.

Taking the analogy of physics a bit further, the last century has seen theory develop rapidly to explain the universe in which we live. In the seventeenth century, Newton came up with a number of scientific laws, most significantly three laws of motion and the law of gravity, that expanded our understanding enormously. However, while Newton's theories worked for the macro world, they did not work for the micro world – so for the atomic and sub-atomic levels we needed quantum physics to explain what was going on (where an object's position and path, and even its past and future, are not precisely determined).

> **Analogy 2.** Old theories, even when correct, may not explain the whole picture. The relevance to business leaders is that we must look deeper into what is happening and try to understand the micro-level as well as the macro, the more random elements (human and energetic values) as well as the neat overview (planning and market dynamics).

I would like to draw one further and final analogy with the world of physics and that is to do with Einstein's theory of relativity. Intriguingly, Einstein was not the first to observe the influence of time and space on the results of experiments. Scottish physicist James Clerk Maxwell, who discovered that light was an electromagnetic wave, identified the speed of light (18 miles per second) and went on to identify different wavelengths such as microwaves, radio waves, infrared light and X-rays, realised that the speed of light was only meaningful if you could identify what this was measured relative to. He unwittingly triggered a huge debate by devising an experiment to test the effect of the ether on the speed of light. This in turn led Michelson and Morley to carry out the experiment after Maxwell's death and conclude that the ether did not exist (the ether had been at the heart of scientific philosophy since Aristotle described it as the substance that he believed filled all the universe outside the terrestrial space).

Many physicists argued for the next twenty years that the ether must exist and that the experiments simply showed that an adjustment to the theory of the ether was required but it was Einstein who finally put an end to the debate with his paper on the electrodynamics of moving bodies. I found this description particularly helpful in understanding the issue of relativity: if an airline hostess is carrying a cup of tea on a plane in the air, is she travelling at 2 mph (walking speed as observed by a passenger), 572 mph (the plane's speed plus walking speed as observed by someone standing on the earth) or 18 miles per second (as it would be seen by someone standing on the sun)?

Analogy 3. The relative picture may give us new perspective beyond the absolute. The relevance of Einstein's theory to business is to do with context. I have sat in many board meetings where we have discussed business performance. Looking back at this, I wonder whether we always chose the appropriate comparisons. The theory of relativity makes me consider what the right view might be – this year's budget (expectation), last year's actual figures (year-on-year growth) or something else. The whole concept of growth as the primary goal may need to be reviewed and perhaps a concept based on corporate well-being given more airtime at board meetings.

The comparison with physics is interesting because it shows us how difficult people find it to accept a new theory. However, I am in danger of digressing too far from the main topic – the idea of introducing a non-mental, non-linear approach to the business world. I am not looking to *replace* the mental approach and, in fact, I will spend much of the book talking about the mental approach. However, as in the case of Newton's work, the mental alone has limitations and does not cover the whole spectrum. As far as I am concerned, in order to extend business theory to cover the whole spectrum of reality, we need to embrace two other 'dimensions' – what one might call the emotional and the intuitive dimensions. Why become stuck in a one-dimensional world when you can live in a three-dimensional world?

Much is currently being made of the Love factor in business. When we love the business we work for or love the brand we buy, we are expressing human nature and at the same time increasing the strong bonds that will contribute hugely to business success. This represents a revolution for businesses and there are still many who shy away from such an idea. Yet the figures are readily available, thanks to research by Bain and Gallup, to prove that this is a powerful idea. Bain's Net Promoter Score measures the level at which employees rate a company as a "great place to work" from 1 to 10, with 9 or 10 suggesting people 'love' working for the company. This has shown there is a strong correlation between the amount of love and the profitability of the business.

The intuitive dimension brings into play the whole body but particularly the gut or 'hara'. This is less talked about than the heart or love factor but equally important. It is, however, more complex. It involves stillness and integrity on the one hand and momentum and group dynamics on the other.

SECTION ONE
THE HOLISTIC APPROACH

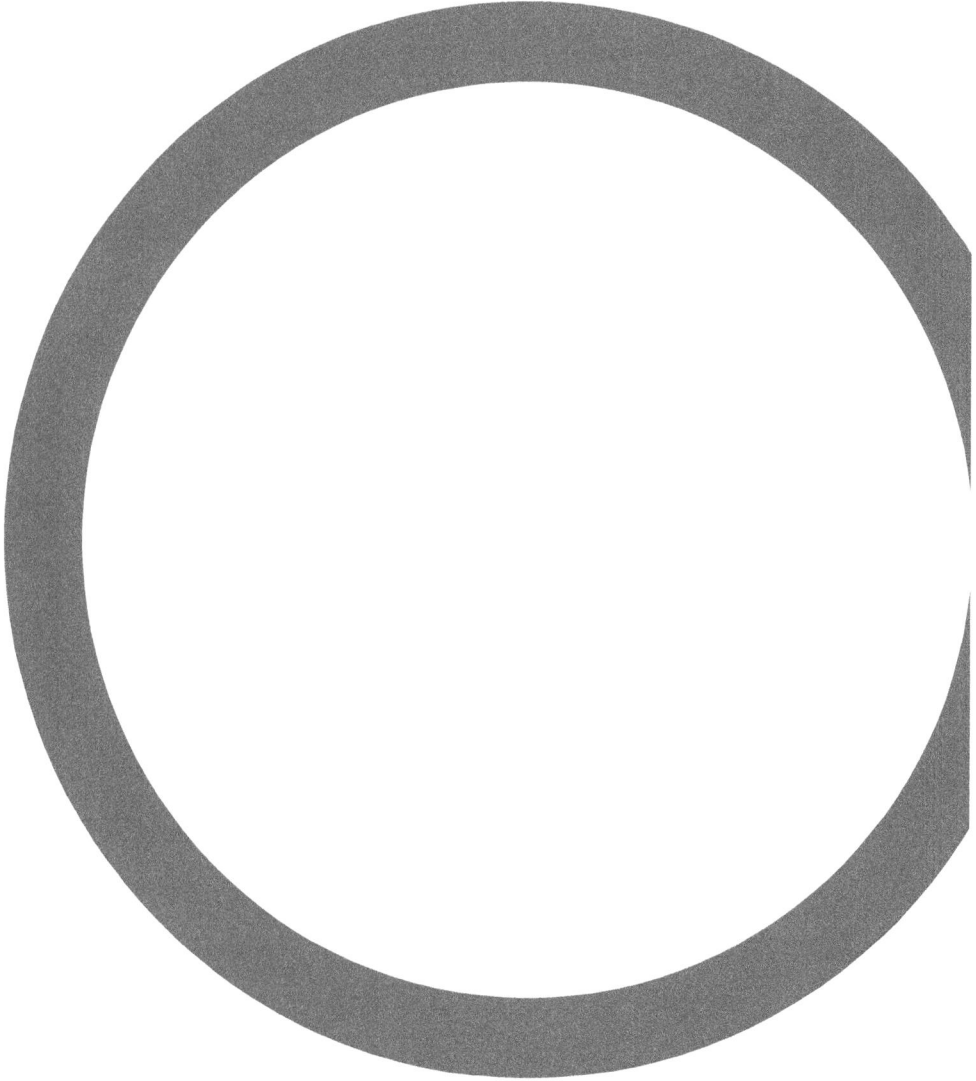

1

EXECUTIVE SUMMARY

Your time is limited, so don't waste it living someone else's life. Don't be trapped by dogma — which is living with the results of other people's thinking. Don't let the noise of others' opinions drown out your own inner voice. And most important, have the courage to follow your heart and intuition. They somehow already know what you truly want to become. Everything else is secondary. Steve Jobs, CEO Apple

The purpose of this book is to introduce business directors and managers to a more holistic approach to planning, defining, developing and running a business. The approach I am advocating is one where the head, the heart and the 'hara' are all involved in the business process.

I am not the first writer to talk about a holistic approach. Tom Peters has quite recently developed a theory on the *Future Shape of the Winner* and describes it as a "holistic approach to excellence". Lou Tice of the Pacific Institute many years ago talked about "holistic organisational development" as a pathway to sustained organisational success. Dave Pollard in his book *Finding the Sweet Spot* identifies three elements necessary for success – Gifts, Passion and Purpose – and states that only when all three are present do you have the basis for success. I would say that this is a holistic theory and relates closely to mine (gifts relates to head, passion relates to heart and purpose relates to hara).

When I was speaking on the platform of the McKinsey Retail Forum in 2004, there was another speaker, one of the directors of McKinsey, who was introducing the idea of "winning hearts and minds" as a way of creating the right environment for significantly better performance. At that time, McKinsey had just been experimenting with a 'people-oriented' approach and, applying it at some of their offices around the world, had recognised that it produced some quite startling improvements.

In September 2010, the Harvard Business Review published findings from some research conducted in conjunction with the Wharton School in Pennsylvania into strategic thinking using managers in an MBA program with some intriguing results. "When we examined the best strategic performers in our sample, we found significantly less neural activity in the prefrontal cortex than in the areas associated with 'gut' responses, empathy and emotional intelligence. Of course IQ-based reasoning is valuable in both strategic and tactical thinking – but it's clear that managers integrate their brain processes as they become better strategists."

The fact is though that these examples of holistic thinking are the exceptions to the rule. Most business theory has been dominated by male, left-brain, linear thinking – not in itself wrong, simply narrow in its approach. The brain is a fantastic workhorse with many facets but it cannot do everything. It will not motivate people on its own – *motivation* comes from the same root as *emotion* and requires the heart to be involved. Inspiration and imagination are also required for a business to be successful and these will only be summoned when we connect not only with the head but the heart and the intuition (which resides in the gut or 'hara').

In this book I take the best of the traditional head-based business theory and then explore how much more effective it is to include the emotions and even take it one step further to include the whole body. I have worked for many years with a theory of three centres – the head, the heart and the hara – that explains how Human beings operate in this world. I expand on this later in the book but my intention is not to give a full description of this theory of human profiling and motivation. My intention is simply to bring a more holistic approach into the world of business and use the 3H (head, heart and hara) or 'holistic' theory as the framework for this.

All business theory covers the HEAD elements – planning, financial model, cash flow, etc. This is necessary for success but not sufficient to achieve it on its own. However, I will start here because it is most familiar for businessmen and therefore easier to access.

There is some business theory that covers the HEART elements – people, motivation, a sense of belonging, etc. This relates to the important matters of external differentiation (what makes your organisation different from other organisations), your brand different from other brands) and internal motivation (each employee's feeling of alignment with others inside the organisation). We are human beings and we are able to make choices. The best people (the talented ones) will be able to choose which company they work for and how long they want to work there.

I have found that very little business theory tackles the subject matter I am covering under the term HARA. The hara represents intuition but it also means the body and movement. Subject matter here includes group dynamics, shared belief systems and the community in business that creates and maintains momentum and flow. When running a business, you may think you have it all covered – the head elements are ok and the heart elements are being looked after – and yet your business is still not successful. In these cases, my experience tells me it will be the hara elements that are the problem – and yet most of us do not even think about this part of our business world.

Using all three centres in business leadership enhances the 'energetics' of a business. To understand what I mean by this, think about a sport and a team you know, perhaps a team you support. Have you ever known a time when the manager's tactics seem right, the selection of players seems good and yet the team keeps losing matches? There is something intangible happening that can explain this phenomenon. This intangible is the team dynamic or team spirit. Something is getting in the way and, no matter how good everything else is, the team will not be successful until it is resolved.

This book is written in four sections. The first section gives an overview of the head, heart and hara theory and a summary of how it integrates into business theory to create a 3 x 3 model for business leaders to follow. The second section goes into the theory of each 'centre' in detail – the head, heart and hara. The third section describes the holistic approach in detail. The fourth section of the book looks at how the integration creates positive energy that nurtures any business that works with the holistic approach.

BIG PICTURE

- HEAD — AMBITION
- HEART — DREAM
- HARA — PURPOSE

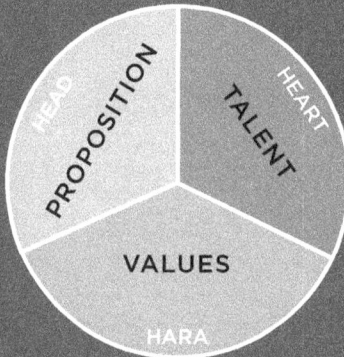

DEFINITION

- HEAD — PROPOSITION
- HEART — TALENT
- HARA — VALUES

GOING LIVE

- HEAD — GOALS
- HEART — ROLES
- HARA — COMMUNITY

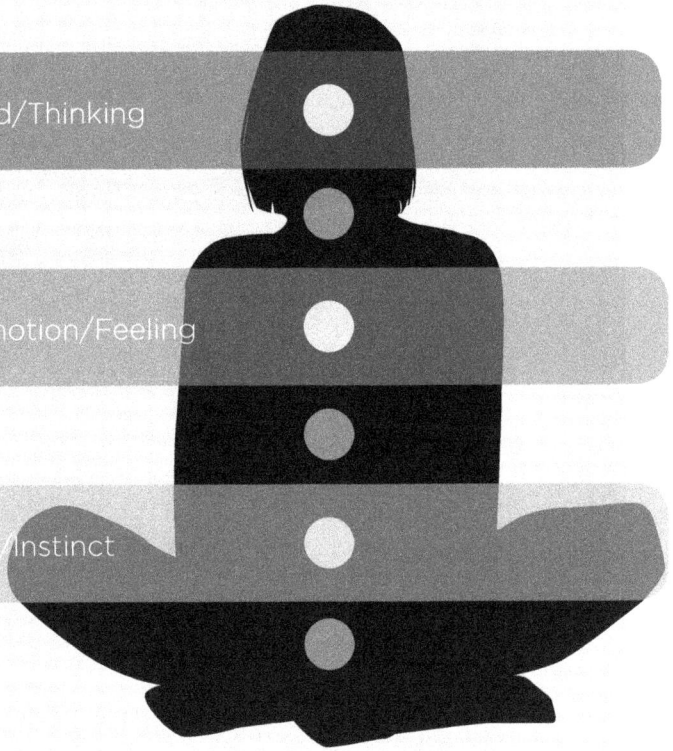

HEAD Mind/Thinking

HEART Emotion/Feeling

HARA Gut/Instinct

2

HEAD, HEART AND HARA, THE HUMAN CONDITION

When you still your mind, open your heart and engage with the movement of the world, everything in life becomes possible.

We come into this world with a package of mental, emotional and physical traits. This is our toolkit for making our way through life and the lens through which we will experience it. And yet most of us ignore many of the tools in the box and consistently pick up the familiar tools instead of the best ones.

I think this quote from Ken Robinson's book *The Element* sums it up well. "We are all born with extraordinary powers of imagination, intelligence, feeling, intuition, spirituality, and physical and sensory awareness. For the most part, we use only a fraction of these powers. These capacities relate to each other holistically. For the most part, we think that our minds, our bodies, our feelings and our relationships with others operate independent of each other, like separate systems". The way I perceive the three centres is directional. What I mean by this is that the way each of the centres operates in different – each one connects with the world in a different way. The head is best at logical linear connections, seeing things in timelines, learning from the past and projecting into the future – so things are either behind you (past) or in front of you (still to come). The heart connects with the world laterally, emanating from you and spreading all around you, linking you to other people in your immediate group and beyond. The hara connects vertically, reaching down into the Earth and up to the Sky, bringing you in contact with the Earth's energy and the Sky's inspiration – all of which fires up your intuition.

The head operates in a linear direction, looking into the past and into the future – this is a masculine orientation.

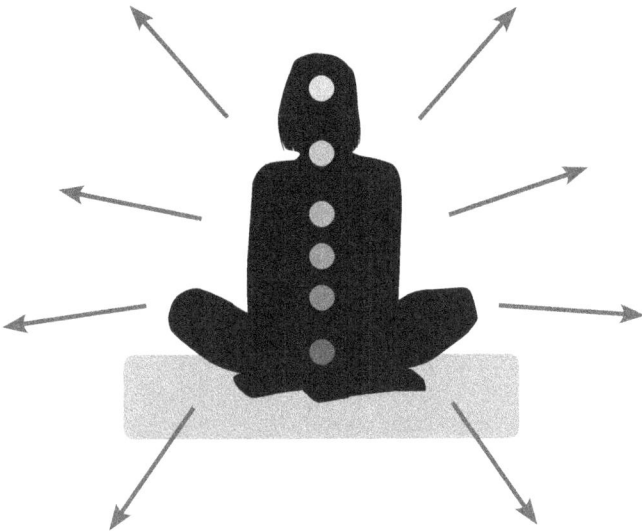

The heart operates in a lateral direction, observing and connecting with all around, this is a feminine orientation.

The hara operates in a vertical direction, rooting itself in the ground on the one hand and connection to the skies on the other – this is neither masculine nor feminine but rather the orientation of the higher self or soul.

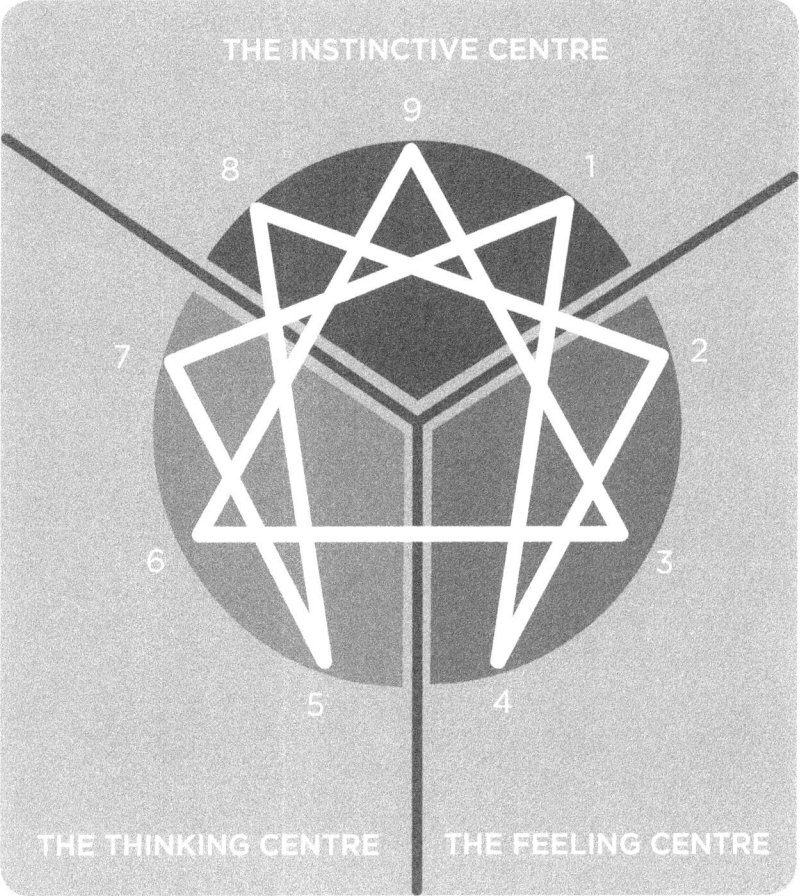

THE INSTINCTIVE CENTRE

9

8   1

7   2

6   3

5   4

THE THINKING CENTRE   THE FEELING CENTRE

The Enneagram

One of the greatest teachers of recent times, G I Gurdjieff, studied the works of the Sufis and many other sources of ancient wisdom. One of the strongest themes of his own teaching involved the understanding that everyone has a tendency to be led by one of three 'centres' – their head (thinking), their heart (feeling) or their hara (doing). He identified three types under each of the centres and showed how each of the resulting nine types has a 'chief feature'. He is generally considered to be responsible for bringing this 'Enneagram' theory (*see opposite page*) to the West.

Gurdjieff used the analogy of a horse-drawn carriage, where the driver represents the head (that chooses your direction), the horse represents the heart (that pulls you along) and the carriage represents the hara (that carries you). Those of us who are driven by the head tend to use that centre to control their lives and avoid things that they fear may happen. Those of us who are driven by the heart centre tend to measure themselves by their effect on others and the feedback they get from others. Those of us who are driven by the hara tend to have an issue with boundaries and become involved in or identified with other people's lives.

In the Enneagram diagram there are nine positions – three in the head (thinking) centre, three in the heart (feeling) centre and three in the hara (instinctive) centre. The typologies that arise are complex and varied by other aspects such as a leaning to one or other number either side, by nine levels of psycho-social responses and even a tendency to behave like a different type under pressure.

I do not intend to go into the personal typologies here. It is a fascinating and enlightening theory that describes the personality and tendencies that you will have as a result of the nature you are born with and the nurture you receive during your formative years. There are many books on the subject if you are interested and I would also recommend that you go to the Enneagram Institute website.

I have taken the three centres as my main influence in developing a new business theory for holistic business. For my purposes here, it is only important that you consider the idea of three different centres and the application of this to the business world.

None of the centres is more important than the others and, while as an individual you may have a leaning towards one of the centres more than the others, I want you to consider including ALL the centres, head, heart and hara, when reviewing and running your business. It is this holistic view that is the most powerful and can lead to a higher level of understanding and performance.

Gurdjieff's key to an elevated life was to be able to 'witness' your own nature and behaviour, rather than 'operating on automatic', and by doing so to be able to shift from a single tendency (driven by head, heart *or* hara) to a holistic level where you operate using all three (head, heart *and* hara) but not driven by any single one. This is key secrets of life and, if you are willing to try to operate using all three centres, it can be the secret to a much more successful business.

3

THE NEW BUSINESS THEORY IN BRIEF

Overview - Going beyond the head

If we run a business we will know about planning and how important it is, although that doesn't mean we all do it of course or that we do it well. How many times have we left the long term to look after itself because of being so busy dealing with the current problems. "I know it is important but is it urgent" was the comment I heard a retail client say once, which sums up how many business leaders feel a lot of the time. But at least planning gets a fair hearing in business – because of course it is the 'head stuff', which is familiar, male-dominated and therefore 'safe'. In fact, there is no doubt that if we did it more and did it better, we would run more successful businesses. However, it is definitely not enough on its own and we need to give as much importance to two other aspects – people (heart) and action (body).

Applying the head, heart and hara theory to business

Theories of business and how to be successful have been expounded many times and in many ways. They are primarily but not solely concerned with the head. I have picked out the strongest and most compelling of these that I have used to guide me as a CEO and as a consultant over the last 30 years. I have reviewed the theories to see how they work in practice. I have also looked back at my experience of real life practice in business to see how if fits the theories.

I have then taken various theories of life path, humanities and belief systems to see where business and life theory combine to form one holistic understanding.

The result is a unique view of business strategy and management and how it can be aligned to the human condition. This creates the platform for a theory that covers both the macro and micro parts of business systems, organisations, markets and development – an overview is captured in the diagram below.

The Holistic Approach to Business

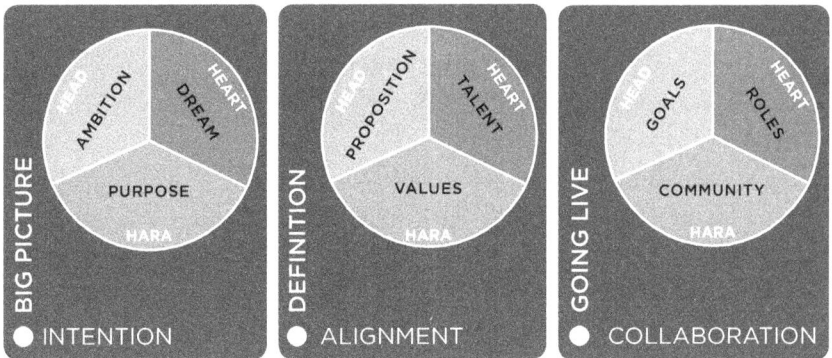

The diagram shows three phases and using the three centres at each phase.

The three phases are in descending order from long-term to short-term:

1 **The big picture** – the vision and purpose of the business – describing the path to be taken.

2 **The definition** – the proposition, talent and values of the business – describing what makes the business attractive (to customers and to employees) and the difference between the business and its rivals.

3 **The living organisation** – the individual goals, the organisational design, roles and responsibilities and the sense of community – describing how the business functions and operates successfully.

3.1 Level One: The Big Picture

Every business needs to have a sense of where it is going – I would call this the Vision. While it is not possible to be sure what the world will be like very far into the future, it is incredibly helpful to have a 'picture' of your business and its role in the future world. It provides a sense of direction and a benchmark against which you can measure your progress year on year. The vision is made up of an Ambition and a Dream. Setting out your ambitions and exploring your dreams are necessary for success but not sufficient. If you are to achieve true integrity – and I believe the real secret to success lies in knowing who you are and what you stand for – you must be clear about your purpose.

Ambition

How successful do you think you can be? What is the ideal size for your business? What reputation can you achieve? What is the quality of your product or service going to be? Answering these questions will help you to identify your ambition. This is necessary for you to reach a degree of clarity that will steer your business growth over the coming years. This can be a 'Big Hairy Audacious Goal' (the 'BHAG' is described in an article in the Harvard Business Review by James C. Collins and Jerry I. Porras) that motivates everyone in the business – for example, a goal like becoming market leader.

Dream

If you want people to be motivated to help you achieve your ambitions you must first share your dream with them. This can be a picture of what life will be like when the hard work has been done and 'nirvana' has been achieved. The picture needs to be painted and the story told in such a way that it fires the imagination of all that see and hear them. It was Jonas Ridderstralle and Kjell Nordstrom in their book *Funky Business* who said it is time the CEO (Chief Executive Officer) became a CSO (Chief Storytelling Officer).

Purpose

Why are you doing what you do? Is there a deeper meaning to what you are doing? Where do you make a difference to the world around you? What legacy will you leave behind after you have done what you do?

Every business has its *original* purpose for starting up in the first place but this may change over time and may need to be reviewed. The *current* purpose shared by management and employees alike is what is required here. This is often more difficult to identify than the original purpose but the process of discovery is a really powerful exercise to undertake with the top management team as the outcome will provide direction and motivation.

3.2 Level Two: Business Definition

Once the vision and purpose have been shared, you are ready to identify the elements that, when put together, will make it a reality – the definition of the business that identifies what makes the business attractive and what differentiates it from the competition. The Proposition will include branding and marketing issues, resourcing issues and structural or financial issues. You need to clarify the sources of income (territories, sectors, customer types) split by product or service types. You have to clarify the ingredients that need to be provided to create each product and service type. You will need to identify the support facilities and functions (premises, finance, administration, IT, etc) required to enable the plan to happen. However, this is the 'head stuff' and is not sufficient to create a successful business. For sustained success you also need to identify your Talent (the team that will best serve your purpose and achieve your dream) and your Values (the basis of all behaviour and expression). For a business that operates as a brand (where the customer relates to the business directly and the whole business acts under one name, such as retailing and service companies) this is also the basis of the brand.

Proposition

Whatever business you are in, you will have customers. Winning customers, satisfying them, ensuring that they come back for more and recommend you to their friends – this is the ultimate recipe for success. To do this you need to know your customers well – and this means an intimate knowledge of the needs and desires of the various customer types you will be attracting. Only then will you be able to ensure that your products and services match the desires and requirements of the customers – the products and services are the most critical part of the proposition as this is what the customer is intent on purchasing. Knowing your customers well will also enable you to create the right buying experience (convenient, inspiring, etc). These days there is a new phenomenon where the proposition is actually a 'platform' rather than a product or service – companies like Google create value and wealth by being part of the lives of a huge community and through this enabling access to that community.

Ultimately, the proposition will lead to a financial business model. Putting all this together and making assumptions about the degree of success you will have in building your business, you can work out the scale and design of your organisation, the resourcing, the space and the facilities and then you will be able to work out how much cash or investment is required.

Talent

There will be a number of factors that influence how the business will do what it does differently to its competitors and these are the result of 'core competence' (skills and knowledge) and the 'core competents' (key people). If you think of any team (try sport if it helps) you will see the impact of the team's combined skills with the influence of the style or nature of the top players – that is what makes them special and makes a winning team successful.

Values

What makes your business different to others? What makes it an appropriate place for one person to work and not another? What attracts your customers and keeps them coming back for more? The key may lie in your products or location but this is rarely enough for true differentiation. The ultimate answer to these questions is 'shared values'. These are the common factors that influence how things are done in the business and drive behaviours. Their effect will be felt through all dealings with customers, all product development and all communication by the business.

3.3 Level Three: Going Live

Once the proposition, talent and values have been established, you are ready to 'go live' – create the business, refresh it or re-create it. This is where life becomes all about detail. You will need a Plan in which the detail is worked out or given as a responsibility to someone else to work out as part of their role in the organisation. You will need to build your Team, being clear about each person's role and responsibilities in your organisation. When you have worked out the plan and shared it with the organisation, you have to do something surprising (and not included in many business books) – 'let go'. Stop trying to control everything and trust the people you employ to do the best they can for the business. This trust creates the environment in which the business will flourish, where people will be motivated to perform to a high degree of excellence while taking care of the Community that is your business organisation.

Goals

A plan ensures that you will have everything you need to achieve your goals. The master plan will need to be broken down into sub-plots, with every department looking at what they will need to provide to ensure the overall plan is achieved. Every goal, at every level, will need a set of strategies and actions to deliver it. The actions of the higher levels will become the goals of the lower levels.

Roles

You need to design your organisation so that it can best serve your goals and strategies. People need to understand what part they play in achieving the organisation's goals. People have a need to build trusting relationships, which can be facilitated by common rules and institutions or systems within the organisation. The system must be fair and recognised as such by everyone. Organisation design is one of the most complex and difficult management tasks there is. If you are lazy about it, however, and do not work through the detail, it will come back to haunt you when your people do not deliver what you want of them because they are not clear what is expected of them.

Community

People are more likely to act in support of the common good if four elements are appropriate for them – institutions, information, identity and incentives. This theory has been developed by Professor Mark van Vugt with a focus on sharing limited environmental resources but I believe it applies equally to any group of people acting in the interests of the whole – and therefore to a business.

Institutions (Trust). People have a need to build trusting relationships and these can be facilitated by common rules and institutions or systems within the organisation.

Information (Understanding). People have a need to understand the physical and social environment as this helps to reduce social uncertainty.

Identity (Belonging). People need to have a positive social identity, a need to belong, and every organisation can help to create a sense of belonging that improves and broadens one's sense of community.

Incentives (Self-enhancement). People need to improve themselves and increase their resources and organisations have to enable this and reward people appropriately to the needs and desires of the group.

In this book I will develop all elements of the model in depth to provide a new and compelling business management theory. Like all good theories, however, understanding all the individual elements is never enough. Towards the end of the book I will outline an additional dimension – that of *Energetics*. Probably my biggest lesson in life is that, as soon as you think you have understood something tangible, you will find there is an intangible element that really has the most powerful effect on your life. Just as you have learned and practiced good theory to the point of excellence, you need to change your approach and think again.

The nature of *Energetics* is such that they are invisible and intangible. If most businessmen find it hard to deal with Emotional elements, they will find *Energetics* even harder. And yet, I can only urge you to persevere. There is no doubt in my mind that it was *Energetics* that saved my business and *Energetics* that made it successful.

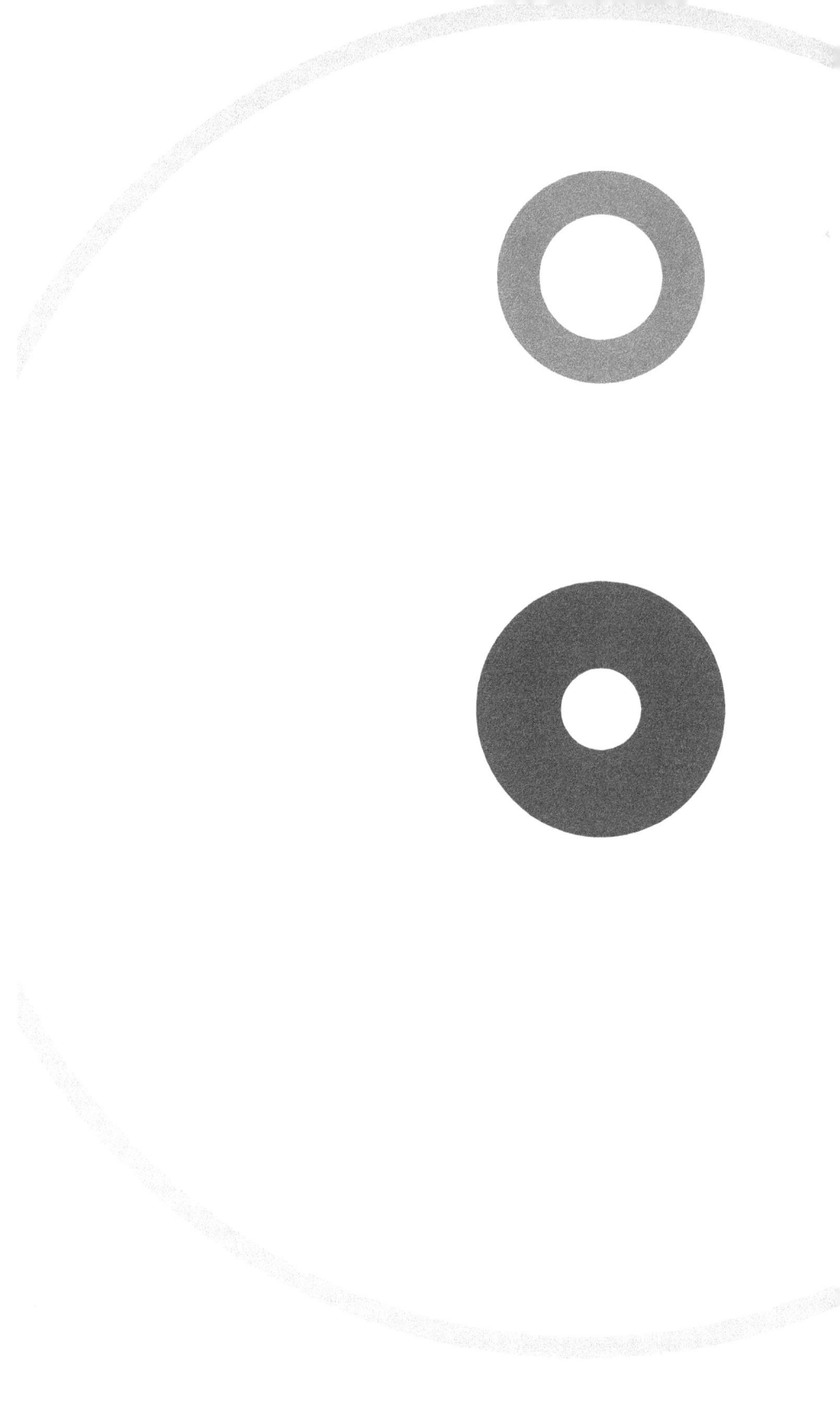

SECTION TWO
THE THREE CENTRES

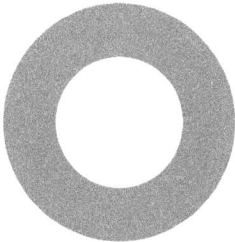

4

HEAD

4.1 Thinking Clearly

What are you thinking about?

People spend much of their lives asleep. I am not talking about the type of sleep where you get into bed, put your head on the pillow, shut your eyes and dream. I am talking about our lack of consciousness while we are apparently awake. There are so many things that we have to deal with every minute of our lives that our brains learn to deal with most of them without bothering our conscious mind in the process.

If you think about the number of decisions involved in simply getting dressed in the morning and yet how little *thought* we give to it, you will get a sense of what I am talking about. We have to decide which combination of clothes to put on (don't think fashion sense or co-ordination for the moment just think about items); we have to decide which order to put them on; do we stand up or sit down to put them on or do we stand for some and sit for others; do we start with the left or right; and so on.

Our brain copes with all this without engaging our consciousness. It is a fundamental of our essential learning process that we start with a lack of experience and gradually shift to *unthinking* activity. This is a wonderful service that our brain provides. It means that we can do many things without conscious thought, which enables us to do other things at the same time. However, there is a danger inherent in this part of our nature.

Some things that deserve conscious thought are relegated to the *automatic* or *asleep* mode. Habits soon form and we hardly notice that we are following the same path again without thinking about it. It is very important that we choose when to be *awake* or *conscious* However, it is one of the hardest things in the world to achieve – so hard in fact that many people believe it is the secret to 'enlightenment'.

Assumption is the mother of all cock-ups

So staying awake is a hugely important concept when it comes to thinking clearly. Another similar concept involves *assumptions*. We all make assumptions and we probably could not get on with our lives without them. However, when something goes wrong (particularly when more than one person is involved) there always seems to be an assumption involved at a key moment that causes us to make a significant error.

An assumption is an example of wrong thinking. "But I thought that you were going to…" is often the cry that goes up when it has all fallen apart. Unchecked assumptions probably cause more heartache than anything else in the world of business. Actions based on wrong assumptions have to be unpicked, time is lost and money is wasted.

Where are you going with this?

You would probably be surprised how unclear we can be in business about the end result we desire and whether the path we are on will lead us there. We get distracted along the way. We lose our clarity as we travel. We may even be surprised when we arrive at a different destination to the one we intended. Setting clear business goals is often a stage that is skipped – and without this clarity we really do not have a hope. Knowing where you are going is a pre-requisite to getting to the right destination. However, even when we have a clear goal in mind, it is surprising how often we lose our way. There are so many distractions and obstacles along the way; there are so many reasons why something was allowed to get in our way and take us off track; there are so many instances of something from left field taking our attention from the original goal.

So, how can we avoid this? The only way I know is by keeping the goal top of mind. This can be done by keeping it right in front of you on the wall; putting in on the desktop of your computer; sending yourself a reminder regularly; or asking someone to remind you.

4.2 Thinking Strategically

Picture your future and plan for it

Imagine you are planning to drive from one town to another 500 miles away. This would not appear to require any great planning and yet look at the list below:

What car are you going to take? You might have more than one car; you might consider hiring a car. This would mean you are faced with choices about petrol or diesel, thirsty or economic, fast or steady, and so on.

What route are you going to take? You could choose the shortest route, the fastest route, the most scenic route, etc.

Are you going to stop? The journey is long enough to consider taking breaks. Are there places you want see along the way? Do you want to stop and eat?

Who is going with you on the journey? As soon as you introduce more people into the equation, the more complex it becomes. Will there be more than one driver – and, if so, how many? Are there a number of different needs and desires to be satisfied? Do some of the party need to stop more often for comfort breaks?

Is the journey part of a bigger plan? If the journey is itself the purpose, you may want to take your time and enjoy every minute of it. If the destination is the most important thing, you probably want to get there as quickly as possible.

When are you going to set off and when do you want to arrive? Where are the sticky points in terms of traffic? Are there cities that will create bottlenecks at rush hour?

There could be many more questions but this gives us an idea of how a plan can be put together to ensure that the journey is as good as it can be. Of course, like any plan, there can always be the unexpected incident (accidents on the motorway that hold you up for an hour) or context (snow and ice on the road). The best you can do is to formulate the plan and then be ready to change it or accept changes beyond your control.

How far ahead are you planning?

Running a business requires you to think ahead. This could be as simple as making sure you employ (or can find) enough people to do the work and enough space for them to work in. It certainly includes making sure you have enough cash to pay for your outgoings and cover the difference between these outgoings and future revenues. Sometimes these things (like cash requirements) are month-to-month decisions whereas others (like premises) are longer-term decisions.

So, what is the right time period to plan for? Nearly all businesses will do annual budgets, focusing on what revenue and what costs to expect in the next 12 months. Many do three-year plans, focusing on how we will grow (or shrink). Some do five-year plans, focusing on how we will develop and shift.

The right time period to plan for is "all of the above" and ideally in reverse order. So, your five-year vision will provide the context for your three-year goals, which in turn will give you the context for your annual budget. There is no way around this process if you want real direction for your business. It is critical for the success of any business to monitor existing and potential markets, review customer trends, track the activities of competitors, review the current proposition and ensure that competitive advantage is maintained or improved in order to maintain or grow market share.

The only exception is when you are planning for survival in a market-place that is not experiencing any significant changes. Survival planning requires you to focus on operational efficiency and a lack of significant change means you can prepare next year's budget based on today's business (current market, current trading patterns and current proposition) without adverse impact on your business.

The concept of three horizons

Picking up on the question asked just now about the right time period to plan for where the answer was "all of the above", one of the neatest descriptions of how to do this was developed by three McKinsey partners, Mehrdad Baghai, Stephen Coley and David White, in their book *The Alchemy of Growth*. The book explains how businesses view, develop and manage three horizons simultaneously.

Horizon 1 is the current business platform, including any potential growth in the current marketplace with the current proposition. The focus here is to extract the maximum revenues, inject maximum efficiency and produce maximum profits while the current business is relevant. A healthy current business is needed to support the development in horizons 2 and 3 – it is described as "earning the right to grow".

Horizon 2 is the next business platform, the emerging business opportunity based around evolution. The focus here is to build the business, grow the revenues, build the resources and invest in new facilities. There may be a case for shifting resources from one part of the business to another.

Horizon 3 is the future business platform, the seed of a new concept, the choice between options and scenarios. The focus here is to review alternatives and choose the best one, define it in detail, identify the investment required and measure the potential future ROI. The new business platform might supplement the existing one or replace it.

Each horizon is progressively more difficult for most directors to cope with. Horizon 1 is the easiest because it involves today's business and therefore a known entity and something that is constantly on the table as a topic of discussion. Even here, however, special effort is required to push the business to its best possible performance but this is within the reach and experience of most company directors.

Horizons 2 and 3 both require directors to find time and space to think about something that does not yet exist and is therefore require theoretical debate. Successful businessmen usually get to the top because they can make things happen – they can see what needs improving and they can motivate people to carry out their wishes. This means that the exploration of horizons 2 and 3 often requires special teams or external specialists who do not have the pressure and responsibility for day-to-day performance and can therefore devote time to open exploration of tomorrow's possibilities.

All three at once

The temptation is to put the planning of future horizons (2 and 3) on the back burner. There is always something about today's business that demands your attention. Tomorrow's business is left till later… "I know it is important but is it urgent". Setting aside time for planning is difficult and is often left far too long – sometimes not done at all.

To quote from the book, "The goal of managing the three horizons… is to develop many businesses in parallel without regard to their stage of maturity". "Managers know that businesses go through different stages of development. Yet most companies are far from having a stock of developing businesses ready to gush out of the pipeline. In many organisations, scant management attention is devoted to some sections of the pipeline while much is lavished on others. Neglecting any horizon at any time weakens a firm's prospects of long-term growth."

4.3 I Think, Therefore I Am

An incomplete theory of Man

Before we leave the chapter on the head, let's consider the bias given to using the head as the leader in today's society. Rational thought is relatively comfortable for us to talk about, particularly in the male-oriented business world. As soon as we start talking about business issues, we seem to give in to an irresistible urge to frame everything in business jargon. Everything becomes 'goal-oriented', involves 'risk assessment' and 'brand positioning' and is measured by its 'impact on the bottom line'.

It all starts with our education. At school we are taught to measure our success in terms of brain-power – how well we remember facts, how well we argue our case, how well we rationalise. Everything is focused "above the neck and slightly to one side" as described in a wonderful talk on education given by Sir Ken Robinson in 2006 (www.ted.com) and developed in his book *The Element*. This has only increased in the last 100 years with the supremacy of science and scientific evidence. And yet our head is only one of three equally important and potent contributors to our capability. The other two are our heart and our body.

Our heart tells us when something rings true. Our heart tells us when someone is being honest. Our heart connects us to higher drivers in life such as passion and compassion. Our heart is the primary driver in decisions about our partners in life. It is emotion not thought that drives us to action.

Then there is our body. How often has a 'gut reaction' led us to a better result than a carefully thought-through rationale? How many times has our intuition (which resides in the gut or the hara) provided us with an answer our head didn't even know about? Have you noticed how your body will tell you when to slow down by giving you a small pain in time to avoid a really big problem?

So, the human condition is a combination of these three operating in unison. Each of us as individual human beings will find that we are more drawn to use one of them before the others. In business we tend to use the head more than either of the others but this is because of training not nature. *For businesses to be most effective they need to learn to use all three centres.* Use all three centres and you will find you are much more successful. Businesses are exactly the same as individual humans. Why shouldn't they be? After all they are made up of groups of individuals operating together.

5

HEART

5.1 Why Emotion Matters

...in a world in which your competitors can copy everything you do, ...all that separates you from (them) are the skills, knowledge, commitment and abilities of the people who work for you..... Companies that manage people right will outperform companies that don't by 30% to 40%. Jeffrey Pfeffer, author of The Human Equation: Building Profits by Putting People First

Personality and emotional intelligence

The greatest influence on the 'energetics' in a business is how people get on with each other. This will depend upon individual knowledge and understanding on the one hand and the business context and values on the other.

Not many people in the Western world are taught emotional intelligence (the intelligence that helps us enjoy good relations with others) so most of us pick it up along the way as best we can. Daniel Goleman has written a series of excellent books on the subject and I would recommend these as a good starting point if you would like to know more. He describes emotional intelligence as "the capacity for recognizing our own feelings and those of others, for motivating ourselves and for managing emotions well in ourselves and in our relationships". It describes abilities distinct from but complementary to academic intelligence. Many people who are 'book smart' but lack emotional intelligence end up working for people who have lower IQs but who excel in emotional intelligence skills.

Daniel Goleman's particular adaptation of this theory includes five basic emotional and social competencies:

Self-awareness. Knowing what we are feeling in the moment and using those preferences to guide our own decision-making; having a realistic assessment of our own abilities and a well-grounded sense of self-confidence.

Self-regulation. Handling our emotions so that they facilitate rather than interfere with the task in hand; being conscientious and delaying gratification to pursue goals; recovering well from emotional distress.

Motivation. Using our deepest preferences to move and guide us toward our goals, to help us take initiative and strive to improve, and to persevere in the face of setbacks and frustrations.

Empathy. Sensing what people are feeling, being able to take their perspective and cultivating rapport and atunement with a broad diversity of people.

Social skills. Handling emotions in relationships well and accurately reading social situations and networks; interacting smoothly; using these skills to persuade and lead, negotiate and settle disputes, for cooperation and teamwork.

Greater knowledge and understanding in this field would be immensely helpful to all businesses yet very few invest in any form of training of this type. This is another example of being led by the head – we are much more comfortable paying for skills training than personal growth training.

But even if all the individuals in a business were emotionally intelligent, the business could still be setting the wrong context and could make it very difficult for the individuals to perform well together. The right context is one where the organisation encourages collaboration and this is the subject of later chapters.

Balancing planning and people. Following up with action.

To be successful, a business needs to balance planning issues and people issues. You need to spend as much time and energy on your people as your planning. You need to get to grips with both the 'hard' issues (head-planning) and the 'soft' issues (heart-people). And then you need to harness the effect of both parts into action – John Harvey-Jones (the ex CEO of ICI) describes this as 'making it happen'. Strong motivation is emotion-based and heart-felt. Our emotions make us act with both speed and intensity. Positive emotions (passion, inspiration, desire) will have positive effect – positive energy acts like a turbo, driving us on faster to achieve the task or goal. Negative emotions (fear, shame, guilt) can also play their part but generally speaking these need to be watched like a hawk because the negative energy, if allowed free range, can stop us from achieving anything – they can 'freeze' us in panic, or 'drown' us in depression.

Many businessmen think that emotion has no place in business and this is probably because they are thinking of negative emotions that get in the way of 'doing the job'. They also may be thinking of emotions as something that has to be dealt with – men in business may not think it is appropriate when a woman becomes emotional or upset about something at work. This is really missing the point entirely but it is perhaps understandable given the frequent use of the word 'emotion' as a negative description.

5.2 Ultimately it's the People that Count

Feng Shui and the Business Bagua

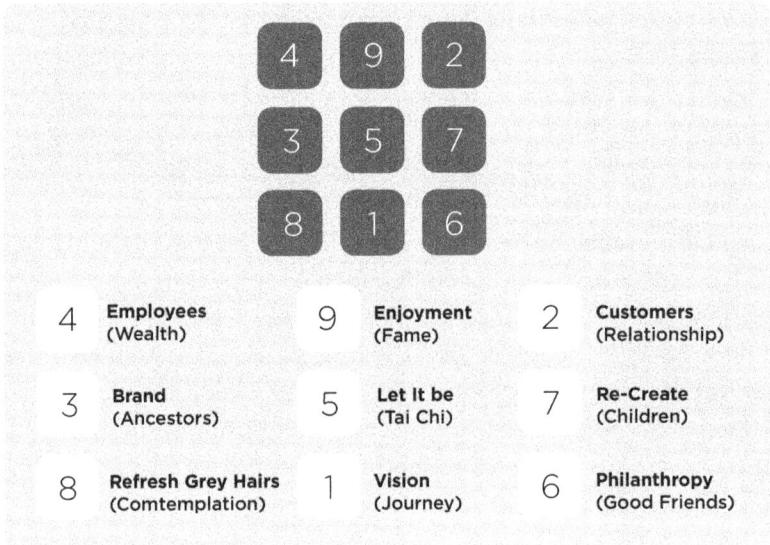

You may have heard of the Chinese philosophy of Feng Shui and how it helps us get the energy flowing better in our homes. Well, believe it or not, there is a Feng Shui for business. This is not just about getting the office space right but provides a nine-point platform for business success called the Business Bagua. Another name for this is the Magic Square because the numbers in any direction always add up to 15.

BUSINESS BAGUA

4	9	2
3	5	7
8	1	6

4	**Employees** (Wealth)	9	**Enjoyment** (Fame)	2	**Customers** (Relationship)
3	**Brand** (Ancestors)	5	**Let It be** (Tai Chi)	7	**Re-Create** (Children)
8	**Refresh Grey Hairs** (Comtemplation)	1	**Vision** (Journey)	6	**Philanthropy** (Good Friends)

The first four elements are quite familiar, almost Western – we are used to developing vision, identifying customers, developing a brand and identifying the resources (employees and other) that we will need to deliver our vision.

The most interesting aspect to me when I first discovered it was the fact that the equivalent of the Wealth Corner (number four in the Bagua and often the most exciting for people using Feng Shui to understand the energetics of their homes) in the Business Bagua is your Employees. It is worth labouring this point a little – your *employees* are the source of future wealth in your business not your cash or even your customer base.

At point five, the mid-point, the Bagua tells us that we need to 'Let Go'. This is unusual for Westerners in business and yet I believe most of us would recognise it at some level. If you have ever been able to observe your behaviour you will know that when you are relaxed and confident everything flows better and you are more successful. The opposite is when you are worried and you hold on too tight and try to control everything.

The most unusual part of the Bagua is the 'back half'. Take a look at what is contained there – philanthropy (give it away or give back), re-creation (refresh and refill), contemplate (enable the founders to take time out to think and re-charge their batteries) and enjoy (the success and reputation you have earned). I would say these are about HEART.

Sharing the dream

You can have the best vision and the best plan in the world and you will fail unless you can align the organisation behind it. The most important group are the leadership team – not because it represents the more senior and higher paid roles but because their influence over the rest of the organisation is so great. If the leadership team is not pulling together the rest of the organisation will sense it and feel uncomfortable and uncertain – and potentially de-motivated and disillusioned.

Leadership team. Getting the leadership team working well is a dual challenge – rational and emotional. The rational side is about skills, knowledge and experience in such a combination that every aspect of the business is covered by the best team you can get. At this level even one bad apple can cause mayhem, so do not avoid the difficult decisions – if a team member has to be redeployed or even replaced you must tackle this straight away.

The emotional side is more difficult to judge but you will sense if you do not have it right. When it goes wrong, you may have two people arguing too often or just a general sense that there is a lack of harmony. If you need help with this there are a number of techniques and consultants who can advise you.

The organization. Once you are sure you have the top team working well, you can focus on the rest of the organisation. It is usual (but not necessarily optimal) for the new vision to be conceived and announced 'top-down'. But it should be remembered that the vision will be delivered 'bottom-up'! Introducing a new vision is a long-term programme and you must communicate it well, with passion, clarity and consistency. You must also communicate it often – more often than you might expect. You may think you have said what you need to say but it may not have been heard. The newer the message, the more often people will have to hear it before they understand and before they can take it on board. It can help to give the project a suitable title and link it to a bespoke bulletin system (print, intranet or internal blogging network). A project champion can also be appointed.

Maintaining the momentum of any change programme requires a great deal of time and effort but without it you will not succeed. Keep telling people the story. Keep them informed of progress. Reward people for taking on board the new behaviours required for the new proposition. Make heroes of people who make a special effort to move things forward in the desired direction. Equally, you must make it clear that those who oppose change will not be tolerated.

Share the programme of change with the business. If possible involve them in the detail, as they will probably know more about it than you do. If involved in this way, they will be much more motivated than if they receive it as a finished plan. This can be done in large groups – processes like Whole Scale and Open Space have been developed for this purpose – or it can be done in smaller specialist groups, say one department at a time.

Report back on progress regularly. Give updates on the results and show how the vision is getting closer to fruition. Introduce new Key Performance Indicators that reflect the new vision, measure them regularly and publish the results so that everyone can see what is happening. This will confirm your commitment to it and will emphasise accountability – it will help ensure that the dream becomes reality.

Customers and advocates

The Heart element also includes the relationship with customers and whether they feel part of your business or loyal to your brand. Relationships are strongest and most positive when built using dialogue – most powerfully face-to-face but more and more these days remotely through the internet and social media.

Recognising this will change the way you do business. Every touch-point with a customer is a moment of truth. It can go well or badly of course but this is in your hands to manage. Every successful business seeks to increase the number of moments of truth and at the same time improve the experience the customer has.

Traditionally, retail and leisure industries have known this and experienced the ups and downs of it. Customers come into their 'space' every day and meet their staff. Depending on the quality and training of their staff, this can be a good or bad experience.

Product and service brands have been less exposed and have been able to manage their brand image and reputation via advertising and other broadcast media. Dissatisfied customers have been dealt with on a one-to-one basis quite discretely. Now, with the internet and social media, every complaint may be shared with a huge audience and so it has become much more important to manage this well – something businesses and brands for the most part have yet to acknowledge. Many brands are also recognising the power of face-to-face contact and building brand centres or consumer experiences in order to win hearts and minds – and ultimately create brand advocates.

5.3 My Own Experience and Experiments

Daring to do different things

If you really want to encourage people to take part in the positive performance of your business, you could do worse than try some things that are unexpected, challenging and even a little scary but at the same time exciting, mind-expanding and energising. Here are a few that I have tried in my own business.

Ocean WhiteHawk afternoon. We invited an amazing spiritual teacher called Ocean WhiteHawk to lead us in an afternoon's adventure just to see where it would lead us. We ended up doing a number of extraordinary exercises, hearing about some inspiring tales and doing some Native American chanting. The result was that everyone had a new and different feeling about the company – it felt more special – and even the cynical amongst us (mostly the men) thoroughly enjoyed the afternoon. Some of the employees went on to do individual work with Ocean in the subsequent months.

Open Space day. Harrison Owen has written about a process called Open Space Technology. This is an invitation for employees to take part in defining and refining the future of the business. The concept is to invite anyone to suggest what would improve things in the business but only if they are prepared to play a role in changing how things are done. Once they have identified the issue and volunteered to be part of the solution, others can add their names to the list to form a group who will work to improve the situation. It only works when the bosses have not already decided what the solutions should be – so it really is 'open' and sometimes frightening for those in charge. However, it is incredibly engaging and therefore very powerful.

Tai Chi mornings. Every year or so I offer to teach a group of employees Tai Chi. At first people may join the group out of curiosity but, as time passes, the ones who stick with it find it gives them something special and brings calm and peacefulness to them as individuals. It is also noticeable that it shifts the energy in the business too – after a session the place seems lighter and the day runs more smoothly.

Recruiting with no job to fill. Yes, I am talking about taking someone on in your business when you do not have a vacancy. While this might seem like a crazy thing to do, I have done it several times and always with a positive result. The reason for doing so has always been that I felt strongly that the person I was meeting for the first time had something special to offer to the business.

Find your own way

There is no one recipe for what is right for your business. I suggest you go and search out new ideas and see if they grab you personally. Then, when you have found one or two ideas you would like to share, start to introduce them slowly into the business. Don't push it down people's throats but offer it as a gift to the organisation. It is not important how many people take you up on it – the people who take part will be the right people. You will probably start to notice small changes in the energy of the business. You may also find more physical changes taking place – some people may leave but they will probably have to leave for their own good and the good of the business. If their path is not your path, their leaving will release energy by their very leaving.

6

HARA

6.1 What Feels Right Probably Is Right

Another word for Hara is gut. In the case of business we talk mostly
about gut instinct. If you are sensitive to such feelings, you may well
have had the experience of 'knowing' that something is right even
when there isn't the data to back you up. A survey in 2010 by Accenture,
the management consultants, showed that 40% of business decisions
are based on 'gut'. Such instincts do not reside only in the gut but can
be felt in many parts of the body. Hence such expressions as "The hairs
stood up on the back of my neck" or "A shiver went down my spine".
Our bodies are a wonderful source of information and guidance,
if we will listen.

Many health practitioners have written about the link between what
goes on in our hearts and minds and what is expressed in our bodies.
Our body will tell us to take a break if we are working too hard well
before our minds will – and if we listen to our body we can avoid the
breakdown that is heading our way.

I have trained in a form of energetic healing – energy is all around us
and I learned to bring that energy through my body, and ultimately
my hands, to provide healing for others. The first time I went to a
session to learn this technique I realised that I would have to set aside
what my mind was telling me because the whole concept seemed kind
of crazy. And, because I wanted to try it, I was willing to do this. After
a while I stopped thinking about it at all and shifted my focus into
'being' rather than 'doing' – using my presence (really being present
in the moment) as an important part of the process. This produced
amazing results.

The same is possible in business. Once you are prepared to go beyond what the mind tells you and learn to be really present, you will be able to tap into this potential by using a combination of *balance* and *flow* (see the next section). To be able to listen to your gut instincts you have to be able to become 'still' – never easy when caught up in the hectic business world. You have to be confident enough to stop running for a moment and sit quietly, almost in meditation, to allow the truth to come through.

If you can achieve this, you will be able to sense what is right. It will allow you to be true to yourself; to act in the best interests of your business without being greedy or controlling (both of which stem from a fearful disposition) and let whatever needs to happen just happen. This is not to say that you sit down and do nothing. It means that you can do the right thing more easily after you have achieved a state of stillness.

If you have ever read *The Inner Game of Tennis* you will understand what I mean (and, if you haven't, you might want to spend a few minutes reading it). The concept of the inner game is to stop the mind trying to work everything out and let the body take over – and in the business world I would say the equivalent is to let your gut instinct tell you what to do rather than your calculating but confused mind. This is particularly true when things are tough because it is in such times that the mind finds it hardest to cope.

6.2 Identifying the Values of the Organisation

Another element of organisations that is linked to the Hara is the fundamental principles, beliefs and values that guide the business.

The business I founded in 1988 is called 20·20 and it is a strategic design consultancy. This means it is built on people providing a service to clients who in turn pay for our time. The time we provide has value because we have knowledge, experience, intelligence and skills that they need – and also because we have a positive impact on them and the success of their business.

Many years ago, we spent a significant amount of time developing the Vision and Values of our own business. We believe that defining one's values is a fundamental foundation for a harmonious and effective business. As Harrison Owen says in his book *How Organizations Transform*, "At the end of the day, the organization will live or die depending on the strength and quality of its values. Is this a place where people care to be, where they feel the freedom to follow responsibly what has heart and meaning for them?"

Our vision has changed a couple of times since we first developed it – this is likely to happen in all businesses because the vision defines *what* you want to do in the future and this will hopefully be ever changing as the world changes and expanding as your horizons expand – but our values have remained the same. In the process of evolving them, we worked closely with a psychologist and long-term business associate, Malcolm Smith, who helped us to develop the values in detail. I think our values at the headline level are quite universal and could be used by many other businesses, so I thought I would share them here.

We identified and developed six values. Three (Brave, Smart and Intimate) described and drove how we behaved; the other three (Balance, Flow and Impact) described what we believed in and strove for.

Since then, partly I think due to a shift in the culture and, in particular, falling standards of parenting and education, we have realised that we cannot take for granted three further values (Clarity, Discipline and Rigour) without which no business can be successful. I consider these to be not so much values as essential ingredients.

Finally, we have identified an over-arching concept for business success, and for life in general, and that is Awareness. This is an over-arching concept because it is transformational and enlightening. I do not see this as a value in the same sense as the first six but more as a way of accessing a higher plane. At its highest level, Awareness is being connected to everything – in a way that everything we do affects everything else.

Behaviours: Brave • Smart • Intimate

The first set of three values are about capability and trust and provide us with a 'way of being' that we can test ourselves against. So we will ask each other whether we were brave just then or whether we were as smart as we might have been? Have we shared openly and collaborated well with each other? We recognise that these three values ask a lot and 'set our style'.

They are challenging and provocative but we like it that way – we even chose key words that are a bit 'in your face' (*brave* rather than courageous, *smart* rather than intelligent, *intimate* rather than open). In order to match these values, we need to bring maximum capability to the table and to be able to trust each other at all times.

Commitments: Balance • Flow • Impact

The next three values are about striving for perfection and represent the 'ideal' that we strive for. I think of *balance* and *flow* as two sides of the same coin – balance being the strength yet stillness required to maintain integrity; flow is moving with perfection and being in the zone. Without balance you are unlikely to find flow; without belief in your ability to achieve flow you are unlikely to find balance.

The third element of this set is *impact* and would appear to be a strange companion for the other two (more practical, less esoteric) until you understand that, while it does include impact on business performance, this is also about seeking perfection by maximising the impact on everyone and everything affected by what you do.

Fundamentals: Clarity • Discipline • Rigour

Next we come to the three essential ingredients we initially didn't think we needed to highlight. These are about performance – individual and group. Without *clarity* we will go round in circles, dissipate our energy and waste other people's time. Without *discipline* we will fail to complete a task, fail to do what others need us to do. Without *rigour* we will not check what we do and will let down ourselves and others with a poor result from our efforts.

When my company were developing our values we made the assumption that such things could be taken for granted but I would counsel anyone doing the same exercise to consider such 'mundane', day-to-day values as being just as important as the 'higher' ones.

Pinnacle: Awareness

Finally, there is the concept that is overarching yet so subtle that we did not see it in the beginning. I described 'awareness' earlier as transformational and enlightening. This is because, once you place importance on awareness, your life changes from one dictated by others into one of free will and choice. When I talk of awareness, I am referring to a consciousness of 'who you are' – of the fact that you are a soul that has taken the form of a human body, that you have for most of your life imitated others and done their bidding, that your behaviour will be dictated by your ego or personality that leads you by the ring through your nose until you wake up to the idea that you have choice.

And, if you are to change this state, it can only start with awareness –
after all how can you change something unless you become aware
of it, observe it and believe that it is no longer necessary to carry on
in the same way as before. "If you always do what you've always done
you will always get what you have always got".

Summary

I have outlined three behaviour values, three commitment values and
three essentials plus an over-arching concept. They all make an
important contribution to the totality of our business but ten 'values'
is far too many to keep in the front of your mind all the time. We
tend to use the first three above all others and check our behaviours
against these on a daily basis.

6.3 My Experience of Being True to Values

The experience of running a business provides one with many tests and many lessons are learned along the way. My greatest test and greatest lesson came when I had to face the realisation that the very survival of my business was threatened through the energy draining away – a 'life-threatening' situation that had to be dealt with swiftly yet sensitively.

When it all started to go wrong

After I had run my business for about ten years, I found someone I thought would lead the company well and recruited him to take over from me as managing director. I felt it was right to step aside, let go of the reins and let him get on with it – after all I carried a lot of baggage as founder and it was time to let someone else bring fresh ideas to the table. Unfortunately, it turned out that I had made the classic management mistake - I hadn't *delegated*, I had *abdicated*.

Over the next few years I probably noticed some things were not quite right but put them out of my mind, not wanting to see the wrong in them. In the end, it was only by keeping in touch with key people inside the organisation that I was able to confirm that things were not right and that something had to be done.

I am not blaming the managing director but I believe that he was wrong for our business because he didn't truly share our values – and, because I had not stayed close to him, I had not given myself the opportunity to influence this.

Making the changes in leadership

The critical moment came when the business was performing badly and we had to make about 20% of the company redundant. I realised at that point that the managing director would have to go too – less because of the poor performance but more for the energetic impact I felt he was having on the business.

I went out for a walk with him and told him I thought I did not believe he was the right person to lead our business. Over the next few days we went for several of these walks until, eventually, he accepted that his future was not with our business. It was a painful process for all concerned. I had to talk to the board and the shareholders about a change of leadership that I saw as absolutely necessary for the business to survive in the long run but which would be very disruptive in the short term.

Rebuilding over three years

I decided the only thing to do was for me to take back the role of managing director and run the business in a totally hands-on manner. Initially I thought I would be able to turn it round in about six months (after all, everyone knew me and trusted me didn't they!!). In the end I found was that it all took a lot longer. Change has to run its course; one big change at the top was not enough and more changes had to take place before we could settle down again to a more stable and profitable future.

We had always retained our staff for a long time – we had built a great team and it was a wonderful place to work. We also had a good reputation in the marketplace and could attract the best talent. However, the previous few years had taken their toll. I wondered if I had waited too long but always believed the business could and would survive. In the next three years many of the 'old guard' left the business and many went on to do great things themselves. Critically there were a few key people who stayed whose belief in the business was as great as mine – and who brought their energy to bear on the situation.

Succession management

After a couple of years I appointed someone from inside the business to be the new managing director of the core business and for a while I retained an overall executive chairman position. This time I stayed close to the managing director and provided help and guidance where

I could – this time I did not *abdicate*. Not everyone agreed with my decision initially but I knew it was made on the right basis this time – my decision was to appoint someone to whom integrity was more important than power. His style and inclination, like mine, was to nurture people and help them develop and grow.

Open space session with all employees

We ran a session of Open Space Technology (see chapter two) and gave everyone the chance to have their say. The rules of the session were:

1. Whoever turn up are the right people
2. Whatever happens is the only thing that could happen
3. Whenever it starts is the right time
4. When it's over, it's over

Anyone who wants to see improvements can put forward their idea and then take part in making it happen. The outcome for our business was a series of small teams set up to bring about the changes necessary. The teams stayed in place for about a year and achieved about 75% of what we had outlined was desirable. This is a far higher level of achievement than most change programmes and it happened because people agreed to make the commitment to making things happen.

Personal development session with key people

Since those days we have maintained momentum around sharing the values through a variety of sessions. One of the things we do is to invite new middle and senior management to take part in personal development sessions that I run at my home. They learned about themselves, their nature and how they related to others. They share and discuss the values and what these mean to the way we do things. Above all they spent time with each other outside the office and felt that each of them mattered to the future health and welfare of the business.

Over time, some of these people have left the business but ultimately that was ok too. We were clear about who were the right people for the future and accepted that some people had to leave. We maintained this clarity about what we needed and why this change (like all changes before it) was simply part of the rejuvenation process – something we needed to go through in order to come out the other side strong and ready for the next phase. Instead of trying to control everything (the traditional, authoritarian, male, head-based and fear-driven approach) we have understood the need to accept that life in business is organic and needs to grow and change.

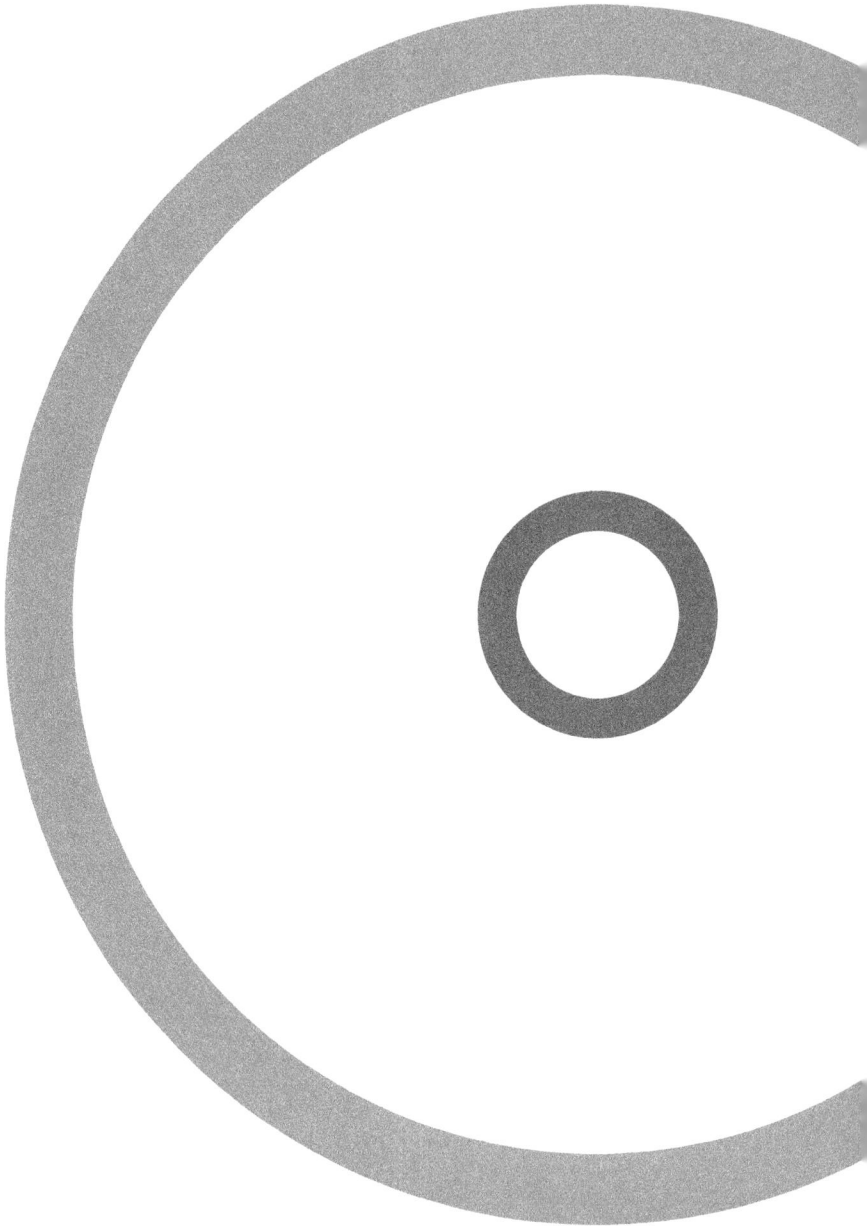

SECTION THREE
THE HOLISTIC WAY

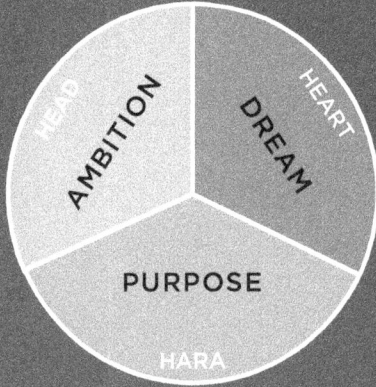

BIG PICTURE

- HEAD — AMBITION
- HEART — DREAM
- HARA — PURPOSE

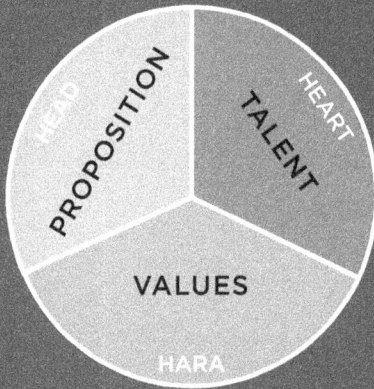

DEFINITION

- HEAD — PROPOSITION
- HEART — TALENT
- HARA — VALUES

GOING LIVE

- HEAD — GOALS
- HEART — ROLES
- HARA — COMMUNITY

7

THE BIG PICTURE

7.1 Ambition and Clarity (Head)

Ambitions

I used to assume that everyone in business had clear ambitions. I always thought that 'professional businessmen' framed their ambitions in terms of how many millions they were going to make – even though my own ambitions were more about 'being the best we could be' than 'making lots of money'.

Now that I have worked with many different CEOs in many different markets, I can see that this is not the case. Some simply add some revenue and consequent profit to last year's figures and this is enough to satisfy the board and the shareholders – they see their job after that being to drive the organization hard (often with a big stick) to achieve the numbers. Others are like mechanics who fine tune their organizations and market positioning to squeeze the last drop out of the current platform. However, every now and then I would meet someone whose ambition extended far beyond this level – someone who would see a real opportunity in the marketplace and who would be determined to 'make it theirs'.

The difference between these types lies in their personality and the degree to which they are a natural 'Talent', 'Manager' or an 'Entrepreneur'. (These definitions come from a book called *E-Myth* and are dealt with at more length in chapter 8.)

Natural entrepreneurs tend to be the ones who see the opportunities and set ambitious and revolutionary goals (perhaps a BHAG – Big

Hairy Audacious Goal – as described in the Harvard Business Review article in October 1996 by James C. Collins and Jerry I. Porras). More traditional manager types tend to set less ambitious and evolutionary goals. Talent-focused leaders will have the knowledge and skill required to do something well themselves but are often afraid or unable to see the big picture.

Developing a vision

A vision can be something that comes to you in a dream while you are asleep, when the imagination is in charge. I believe it is possible to dream up a vision while fully awake. However, people often find it hard to develop a vision. If they don't already have a dream or clear ambition, they don't know where to start.

There are many definitions of 'vision', and probably as many as books on the subject. When I talk about vision, I am referring to a description of where you want the business to be in say three, five or even ten years' time which motivates you and the whole business to strive to go there.

At one end of the spectrum it must be driven by ambition – the ambition of the owners and leaders of the business – an expression of a goal. This can be defined in a number of different ways:

> **Scale and growth** "We want to double the turnover in 5 years"
> **Market share** "We want to increase our market share from 15% up to 20%"
> **Beating a key competitor** "We want to kill the enemy"
> **Reputation** "We want people to think of us as the best"

At the other end it must be driven by what is possible and by what is appropriate – a link to reality. This is about knowing who or what you are as a business – what you are like (your nature), how you behave (your culture), what you are good at (your competencies) and what you are known for (your credibility). Building a business around a vision can only be successful if you take account of the internal

BRAND PLATFORM

NATURE   CREDIBILITY

CULTURE   COMPETENCIES

FOUNDATION

context (building on your roots or foundations) and external factors (your brand platform and market conditions).

It is very hard to sit down on your own, in isolation and dream up a vision and you may need to bring in specialists who can help you by employing a number of techniques – using examples of clear visions used by other companies, challenging interviews, open-minded workshops and gap analysis.

There are many good examples of company vision, like Sony's famous ambition to re-frame people's perception of Japanese products or Henry Ford's ambition to make a car affordable to the masses. Such examples can be very helpful when deciding on the 'type' of vision appropriate for your business.

Taking the key players in a business and subjecting them to challenging interviews is a good way of stretching the mind, raising the bar, shifting the horizons – in other words starting to change the mindset of the leadership group in your business.

Workshops or brainstorms can be run at many different scales – they sometimes involve only one person (the CEO), normally they will involve the core leadership team and occasionally they can even involve the whole company. The choice is usually at least initially dictated by the leadership culture - the way things are done around here. The more people that are involved, the more time you will require for the process – but the greater the motivation (and therefore positive impact on the business). Ideally you will set aside several days for workshops – this will allow you time to do the job properly, in which case you should not have to repeat the exercise for several years.

Finally, gap analysis is a way of seeing the size of the 'jump' you are about to make so that you can put in place the programme necessary to achieve it. The gaps that are generally measured include Credibility (reputation), Capability (competencies), Resources (people, technology, etc), Culture (nature and 'will') and Brand (platform stretch and branding structure).

Evaluating a vision

Once you have dreamed your dream and articulated your vision, you need to decide whether it is achievable or not. Even if it is achievable, you must decide whether it can be built on your current business platform and market position. If not, you need to decide where are you going to look for growth and how are you going to choose the best route. Evaluate what is happening in your market. Is there natural growth in demand for your type of products and services? Is there a danger that your market will be affected by a threat lurking just outside your current market such as new developments and technologies, customer lifestyle changes, etc?

Then have a look at your competitors and see whether any of them have a 'soft underbelly' where you can move in on them and take market share – and whether this additional market share is enough to achieve your growth plans.

Is there a unique platform available for you to create a 'temporary monopoly' (as Jonas Ridderstrale and Kjell Nordstrom call it in *Funky Business*) or a moment of 'surpetition' (as Edward De Bono describes it in the book of the same name). What is this? It is the opportunity to invent a product or service, or some important element of it, or re-shape consumer demand for the products or services in your market – and by doing so grab (create) a slice of the market in which temporarily no competitor exists (until someone copies you).

Where do we look for growth?

If you find that you cannot achieve your ambitions with your current business platform, you will need to look around for opportunities to grow. This will mean considering new markets (customer groups, product or service sectors), new products and technologies (inventing new market opportunities or redefining existing ones) and new territories (geographic expansion – national or international).

Some of these will be easier for the business than others in terms of market entry. Identifying strengths and competitive advantage that in themselves present a barrier to entry to the competition is key. Try to avoid going for routes that involve more than one 'shift' at once (like a new customer group and a new product at the same time). A further consideration is the ability of your brand to stretch with credibility into new markets. Don't assume any market or territory will be easy to enter for the first time – just because a market is large it doesn't mean there is any room for you in it or that competitors will move aside to let you in.

Which is the best route?

You will also have to give serious consideration to whether one growth path is more suitable than another. So often a business chases after an apparently good market opportunity only to find they fail due to a lack of 'fit' between their existing business and the new one. So, once you have identified potential opportunities, you must test these out against your brand platform, your organisation's competitive strengths and weaknesses; and a measure of the market attractiveness against your existing market portfolio.

There will be high risk and low risk options but arguable the best route for growth will be one that optimally balances the market opportunity with the company's capabilities, experience and culture. The only consistent truth is that, like water, you want to follow the easier, smoother path to success. When comparing two avenues it is usually fairly clear which one will provide the greater success. Whatever you decide to do, try to build on your current and core strengths. See if you have something unique to bring to a new market and make sure that there is latent demand for what you bring.

Finally, before going ahead, there is a need to consider whether or not to pursue any of the paths you have reviewed. Sometimes the most difficult but right decision is not to go for any of the selected paths but perhaps to revise your vision, be less hasty and patiently await the next good opportunity. Sometimes the best advice is "Don't" or "Wait".

In pursuit of a vision - the big questions

To help businesses make the right decision about the pursuit of opportunities for growth, I suggest you ask four questions. Is there a good opportunity; is it worth trying; can we do it and should we do it?

Can we identify a good opportunity? There are three levels or types of opportunity that can be considered: brand new markets; re-invented markets; existing markets. You may be an inventor or employ inventors (scientists, engineers, technicians) whose task it is to discover new products. If so, this could enable you to 'create' a brand new market based on a brand new idea or invention. In recent years, new technologies have been developed that have created a new market (demand from a consumer group that did not previously exist) – and at the same time often destroyed an existing market. Re-inventing a market is another option. What does this mean? In many markets things have been done the same way for many years – and often to the dissatisfaction of the customer. Re-inventing the product or how the product is sold and supported can produce powerful change in a marketplace – it can bring about a paradigm shift. For this reason it is worth seeing as something different to simply 'competing better in an existing market' and it is worth investigating as a platform for achieving your vision. In reality there are very few occasions when a good business opportunity is discovered that no-one else has thought of. So, for the most part businesses grow through competing better in an existing market. When measuring the potential of an existing market, you need to look not only at the size and value of a market but consider how you can grab market share. This is only going to come from a competitor, so the questions you need to ask are: "Who has a soft underbelly? Which of the current players in the market can we grab business from? Whose customers can be persuaded to move to a new offer?" It is important that you are realistic about this.

Is it worth doing? This is where ideas give way to measurement – designing metrics that allow a board of directors to make a considered, value judgment. Yet how can you measure the future? Well, this requires a good understanding of consumer motivation and behaviour, a knowledge of trends and an ability to make predictions and projections. The more novel the market situation and the more radical the level of change, the more difficult this is. Research can help but it is notoriously difficult to research the future and the 'not yet experienced'. Scenario development and planning plays a key role in this phase whereby the chosen future is overlaid on alternative scenarios and evaluated for risk and reward. The most difficult, and yet the most important, aspect is to project the future level of demand for a new or re-invented product or service in each scenario. This requires the application of the right blend of experience and intuition to the evaluation of each. At this point the chosen path or strategy can be financially modeled and the potential ROI assessed and a risk/reward evaluation completed.

Can we do it? Most businesses will find that there is a natural and finite limit to their scale potential determined by a number of factors.

These limiting factors are market forces, resources available, skills and training limits and even the type and size of 'frame' you put around your picture of the business. If you have the appropriate experience, you may be able to determine this for yourself. More often than not you will need to employ outside consultants to help you discover the growth limits of your business. What you are primarily looking to determine is whether or not there is the capability and the will inside the organisation to achieve the vision – and if it can be done without unacceptable distraction from the performance of current core business.

Should we do it? How big is the potential gain and how much will it hurt to get there? Ultimately that is the question to answer before going ahead with the plan selected to achieve your vision. Will the gain be worth the pain? Pain can be expressed as risks including external forces and unforeseen changes, internal factors and organisational and management disruption. This downside must be calculated and an assessment made that the business and leadership can manage it. If all your answers are sufficiently positive to outweigh the risks then you can set off in pursuit of your vision.

Strategy evaluation – in pursuit of growth

Assessing opportunities and risks and deciding whether or not and how to act is something we do every day, whether it is crossing the street or buying a house. In business innovation it is no different but it is complex enough to require thoughtful process.

Research. What are we trying to measure? Well, the first thing to measure is the scale of the opportunity. This is the most difficult because it relies on identifying and assessing the scale of demand for something that, at some level, does not exist. Consumer research can be used but not traditional forms of research for there is no data about the future. However, we can find out about consumers preferences, needs and desires and from this information we can try to predict or at least extrapolate what might happen if they were faced with a new choice.

Analysis. If we are dealing with an existing market, we can measure the size of the relevant sector, see which competitors have what slice of the market currently and work out what we could take from each competitor. To do this we will need to assess the strength of the new proposition relative to the competition and at the same time the propensity of the consumer to change.

Measuring the gaps. There are four main 'gaps' we need to be able to identify: capability, culture, brand and credibility. The size of the 'jump' will determine the chances of success.

Capability is an internal measurement based on the core competencies of the business (and particularly the leadership) and the skills and the knowledge in the business. It can also be critical how widespread the capability is across the business – if it resides in one or two individuals this may be enough or it may be a flaw in the plan, depending upon how easily the capability can be shared and learned. If it doesn't exist inside the business, how easy is it to acquire.

Culture is the way the business operates – "how things are done around here". If the business culture is traditional, authoritarian and risk-averse, there will be an inevitable problem asking the business to make a big shift in the proposition as there will be a great deal of resistance – perhaps so much that it cannot be overcome.

Brand is established primarily through customer perception, built via communication and behaviour, and through customers' actual experience of using the product or service. It is also established through 'community' or "advocacy" – where those who feel strongly in favour of or against a brand will tell others about it. Any new proposition will need to be reviewed for alignment with current brand positioning.

Credibility is established by proving quality, knowledge, etc and is built on customer experience. Businesses and brands cannot easily introduce a new product or service under their name unless the customer can feel comfortable about the brand stretch – "Is it plausible for this brand to introduce this product and do I believe they will do it well?"

Investment analysis. To achieve your dream and reap the rewards, you will need to invest – that is invest money, energy and time.

Investing money. The most obvious investment is the financial one – from cash flow, reserves, equity or borrowing. There will be a number of parties who will need to be carried with you, such as the shareholders, the bank manager, the venture capitalist or whoever has a stake in the outcome. What they will all want to know is, "What are the risks and what return can we expect on our investment?"

Investing energy. A less visible investment is that of Energy – human energy. Even tough we know that "if you always do what you've always done you'll always get what you've always got", sticking to the status quo is a great deal easier than developing a new proposition. New propositions demand breakthrough activity, which is both stimulating (positive energy) and stressful (negative energy). The leadership team will feel this the most but everyone who is affected by the change will in some degree or another have an attitude towards it and their response will affect the success of it either positively or negatively.

Investing time. One of the biggest (but often forgotten) investments is that of time. It is very important to acknowledge how much time will need to be invested in the development of a new proposition and where that time will come from. It is critical to identify what impact this will have on the areas of the business that will have less time attributed to them as a consequence and if necessary to buy in additional human resource and take account of this expense in the ROI evaluation.

7.2 Dreams and Pictures (Heart)

At the Big Picture level the heart centre is mainly about pictures and stories. To engage the heart, we need to paint pictures. To provide a common culture we need to tell stories. It has always been this way and always will – because humans are driven by emotion. It is 'e-motion' that creates movement. It is passion and compassion that have throughout history created the platform for major social change – for social or political 'movements'.

Pictures and stories can kindle such change and are also needed to keep it going. If the leaders stop telling the stories and painting the pictures, the followers will stop believing in the desired future or will no longer be prepared to work hard to make it happen.

It's all about love

When we love something we will put a lot of effort into nurturing it and caring for it. We will speak of it in glowing terms and recommend it to others. We make time for it and we enjoy the time we spend on it. This is equally true of a sport we play, a brand we buy or a company we work for.

Research has shown that people's view of their job works at one of three levels. At the lowest level there is a job that pays the rent ("I am doing this because I have bills to pay"); at the middle level there is the job that represents a step on the career ladder ("I am doing this because it will help me get the job I really want in the future"); at the top level there is a job that is a vocation ("I am doing this job because I love it"). While I do understand that there will always be these three attitudes, I also believe that an employee in any of these mindsets can still love the company they work for while they are there.

Other research has shown that successful companies go the extra mile for their employees and, in turn, their employees go the extra mile for the customers.

Persuading people

Stories are often told to persuade people about something – so, in business, who has to be persuaded? Clearly the investors are key, as without their money it will not happen. Equally the leadership team has to be as one on the vision and the potential for the new proposition to be successful. For these two audiences the proposition must be well-defined, the potential well-measured and business case well-argued. Remember, however, that these groups are made up of human beings – so make sure the story is well written and exciting too.

For the employees in the organisation the storytelling is even more important. They are not risking their money and they are not part of the decision-making team. However, they want to feel they are part of a business that is moving forward positively and will be successful – whether they have an active part to play or not. Storytelling is incredibly important in motivating employees and helping them to feel they are 'in the right place'.

Using pictures to evoke statements

When developing key statements to describe your business and what makes it different – perhaps in a workshop situation – it is very helpful to use pictures. People often struggle to know and describe their 'essential self' and, because they work at the emotional level, pictures can release such descriptions more easily. A few years ago I was working with a very restrained group of directors who were finding it really hard to describe their business. I spread out about a hundred pictures on the table and asked them to choose three each that they felt captured the essence of the business. They were given very little time to do this so the head did not play too big a part in the choice. They found this surprisingly easy to do. I then asked each director to describe why they had chosen each picture and they were able to find the words they previously struggled to find.

From this collection of descriptions we developed a common language that everyone was able to agree on and this process too was made much easier by the fact that the descriptions were endorsed by the pictures used to trigger them in the workshop, which gave the words more credibility.

7.3 Purpose and Originality (Hara)

Why are we in business?

At the Big Picture level the intuition and the (corporate) body centre is about knowing why we are in business – what sense of purpose we share with others that makes us special. It is surprisingly easy to get this one wrong. Not many businesses are well connected to their purpose (and I don't mean "making money for the shareholders") and yet this is perhaps the most important element of the Big Picture. Apart from making money, what drives our daily routines and decisions? What gets us up in the morning and motivates us to do it day after day?

A shared sense of purpose can be derived from many different things. It helps if these are positive ones: doing something for the community, making people's lives better; introducing new technologies. It is not that we have to speak about such things every day but that we know that we have this purpose in common and we are doing what we can to the best of our ability to bring about a successful outcome.

David Packard of Hewlett Packard gave a speech in 1960 to HP employees about purpose:

"I want to discuss why a company exists in the first place. In other words, why are we here? I think many people assume, wrongly, that a company exists simply to make money. While this is an important result of a company's existence, we have to go deeper and find the real reasons for our being. As we investigate this, we inevitably come to the conclusion that a group of people get together and exist as an institution that we call a company so they are able to accomplish something collectively that they could not accomplish separately – they make a contribution to society, a phrase which sounds trite but is fundamental. You can look around [in the general business world and] see people who are interested in money and nothing else but the underlying drives come largely from a desire to do something else: to make a product, give a service – generally do something which is of value."

Examples of purpose statements

It is probably helpful to look at examples of companies' purpose statements to give an idea of how other people do it.

Apple: To bring the best personal computing experience to students, educators, creative professionals and consumers around the world through its innovative hardware, software and Internet offerings.

Google: To organize the world's information and make it universally accessible and useful.

Skype: To be the fabric of real-time communication on the web.

Amazon: To build a place where people can come to find and discover anything they might want to buy online.

Microsoft: To enable people and businesses throughout the world to realize their full potential.

Sony: To experience the joy of advancing and applying technology for the benefit of the public.

3M: To solve unsolved problems innovatively.

Hewlett-Packard: To make technical contributions for the advancement and welfare of humanity.

Walt Disney: To make people happy.

Wal-Mart: To give ordinary folk the chance to buy the same things as rich people.

Nike: To experience the emotion of competition, winning and crushing competitors.

McKinsey & Company: To help leading corporations and governments to be more successful.

Originality

As human beings we are all different. Some of us enjoy this and happily stand out from the crowd. Others do not want to and do their best to meld into the average. In business it is very important to be different and to be seen. This means you have to stand for something – which in turn means you have to show positive support for some things and just as clearly reject others. Through these decisions you create your identity and through consistency you show your integrity. All of this individuality and originality is related to your sense of purpose.

Momentum

When you set up a business, you inevitably have a high degree of motivation but not necessarily a great deal of momentum. Momentum is achieved by creating products or services, finding customers who want to buy them and building a reputation among the customer community that helps demand for your products or services to grow. At the same time, your reputation will also attract people who want to join your business and become your new employees. Momentum is essential for a business – just like it is for a human body. Being a couch potato is not good for a human body and being a sluggish business has the same effect. Growing the scale of the business is the traditional way of achieving momentum but in today's world we may well have to look for other ways.

The nature of change

Change is a constant factor of our lives and yet it is something we never quite get used to. Innovation is necessary to make progress in this world and to continue the process of evolution. Being the first to produce something new can be a route to creating a successful business. If we don't change we stagnate. Standing still is not an option in business – you either move forward or your move (relatively) backwards because, if you are not moving and everyone else is, you will be left behind.

If there is a better way of doing something, it would surely be crazy not to adopt it. If customers are doing things differently you cannot ignore it and expect them to use your product when it is no longer relevant.

Change requires willpower. There is enormous resistance in everyone to change – even those who think they welcome change, if they are being honest, will acknowledge this. So you have to judge whether the business has the will to enter a new market, develop a new product, build (or rebuild) a brand reputation in the market. Equally you will need to judge whether the business has the will to change its internal behaviours, restructure and take on new roles, and so on.

All such changes are disruptive and tiring. All your people will have to be highly motivated if they are to maintain the momentum required.

There is an equation about driving change through an organization that explains why it is so hard and it is all about overcoming resistance:

$$D \times V \times F > R$$

D Dissatisfaction   **F** Positive First Steps
V Vision   **R** Resistance

Dissatisfaction with the old world order and Vision about the new world order and Positive First Steps all have to be in place to overcome the natural Resistance that we all have to change in our lives. If any of these factors is rated at zero, the change will not be achieved (hence the multiplication signs in the equation) and resistance will win the day.

8

DEFINING THE BUSINESS

8.1 Propositions, Customers and Markets (Head)

What is a proposition?

At its simplest, a proposition is an offer one person makes to another that can be accepted or rejected. As a business, in order to make sure that your proposition has the best chance of being accepted, you need to understand your customers' needs and desires so that you can tailor your offer to your target customers. So, if the British customer likes crisp and sweet apples, you will need to supply an apple to fit that taste. The relationship between the offer and the customers' needs and desires is the horizontal axis of the proposition model I developed and have used for about ten years (see following page).

How the customer accesses the offer is probably one of the elements that has changed the most in the last few decades, particularly with the internet, and the customer experience is now much talked about these days. In their book *The Experience Economy*, Joseph Pine and James Gilmore talk about how, after the second world war, the bare products were all the customer was offered and how over time this was followed by them being packaged and then branded – with a latest phase where the whole experience of buying the product has become the ultimate product enhancement. This is the subject matter that belongs in the top of the proposition model.

The brand or business that develops the offer for the target customer in the various environments sits in the bottom part of the model. Here we are dealing with the history and capabilities of a business, along with the reputation and credibility of the business.

The proposition model

When I first developed my proposition model *(see opposite page)* it started as a way of constructing retail propositions. For this reason it was developed to include the selling environment and the various channels involved these days. For the same reason it included the customer as part of the model (quite an unusual idea for most brand or business models) – after all the customers walk in and out of the environments that retailers operate. Now it works just as well for product and service brands who have begun to have more and more direct contact with customers through their own channels and new media.

The customer

In this section we are dealing with the 'head version' of the customer – the definition not the relationship. By this I mean that we look at an analysis of all consumers, separate into different groups (by age, disposable income, etc), identify different mindsets (by need and desire, influences, knowledge and experience) and, with this information, decide which groups in what mindsets are the most likely to want to buy from us.

This will help us to tailor our offer to them and ensure that the shopping environment enhances the experience. If we are dealing with customers in a variety of mindsets (which is likely) we must understand how they differ and help our employees deal with each customer type appropriately.

Markets

Each group of customers is a different market. The group will probably be defined by gender, location, wealth, ethnicity, religion or whatever is the relevant set of 'absolute' elements in their lives when they are considering purchasing your offer. Critically, you will need to understand what other offers they will consider purchasing and from whom. You will need to make sure that your combination of product features and benefits, brand perception and price will be enough to persuade the

PROPOSITION MODEL

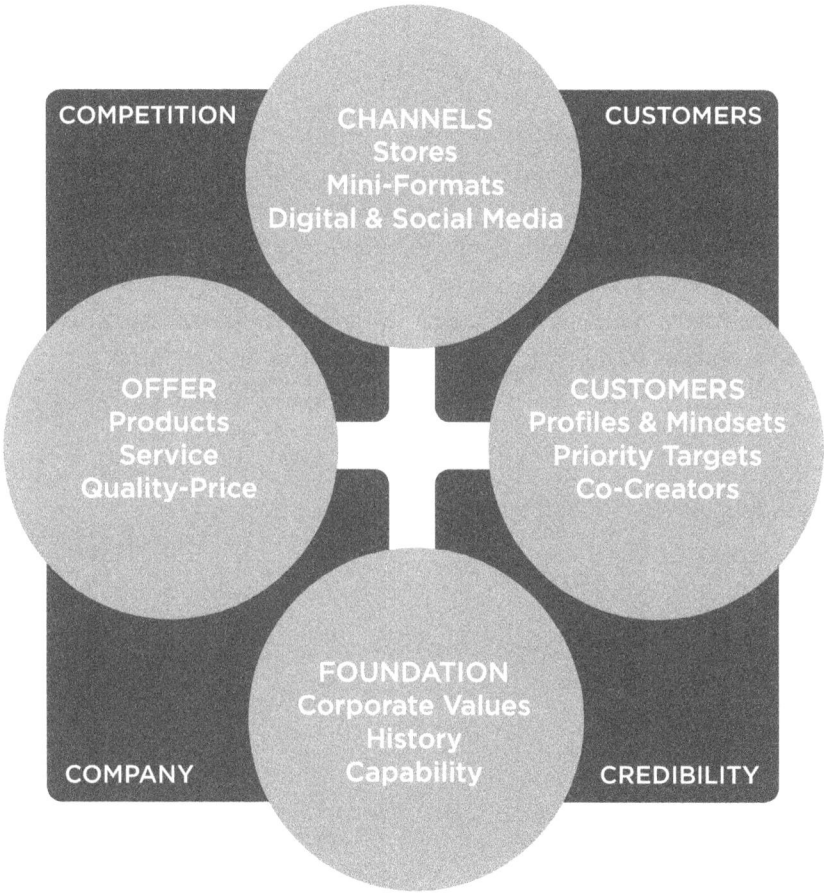

COMPETITION

CHANNELS
Stores
Mini-Formats
Digital & Social Media

CUSTOMERS

OFFER
Products
Service
Quality-Price

CUSTOMERS
Profiles & Mindsets
Priority Targets
Co-Creators

FOUNDATION
Corporate Values
History
Capability

COMPANY

CREDIBILITY

customer to choose yours and, alongside this, you must realise that the shopping journey will also influence the choice (time and distance, enjoyment, etc).

Financial model

Every business has to determine how it is going to operate and at what scale. There will be an optimum size for every business where profitability is high because the revenues are achievable, the team is efficient and the overheads are in balance. It may be small and local or big and international. Likewise, the way it operates may vary between relatively fixed with permanent staff or more flexible with freelancers used according to the type of work to be done at any one time.

8.2 Talent and People (Heart)

People businesses

The businesses I have run have always been 'talent' businesses. Consultancy is a service business that relies on its people to provide much of the value that clients pay for. Intellectual property, such as the proposition model just described, is important but will be worth little or nothing without talented consultants to apply it. The biggest contributor to success is the quality of the people who represent the consultancy and the quality of the relationship they nurture with their clients.

One of the best books that deals with this is *Aligning the Stars* by Jay W Lorsch (Harvard) and Thomas J Tierney (Bain). It is a book about professional service firms (PSF) and is based on a study of 18 consultancy practices from management consulting to accountancy and from the law to advertising. They identify that the tension between institutional strategy (a firm's goals and decisions) and individual strategy (a professional's goals and decisions) is an inherent characteristic of the PSF business model.

Ultimately, it is the behaviour of stars in the context of their client and firm relationships that determines the efficacy of the firm's strategy (see diagram below).

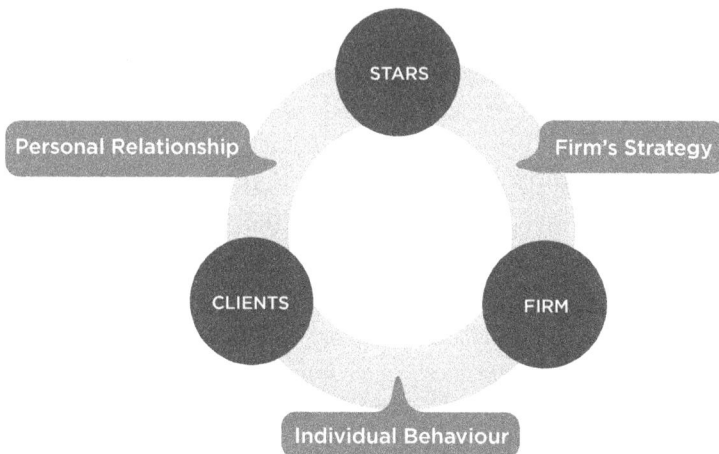

STARS

Personal Relationship

Firm's Strategy

CLIENTS

FIRM

Individual Behaviour

However, it is not just consultancy that needs to recognise the importance of its people. All businesses need good people and will succeed with better people. In *Funky Business* they developed the phrase 'key competents' instead of the traditional 'key competence' – in other words the people rather than the skills. In Tom Peters recent work he has put the emphasis on Talent, which sits right at the heart of his *Gyroscope* organisational model. The model has three facets: ambition-performance, brand-experience and architecture-execution – and each has talent at the centre to make it effective.

In a fascinating book about groups that had performed to an extreme level, called *Organising Genius*, talent is again identified as critical. The leaders of great groups love talent and know where to find it – they revel in the talent of others. However, it was also identified that talent must fit in. Certain tasks can only be performed collaboratively and it is madness to recruit people, however gifted, who are incapable of working side by side towards a common goal.

Of course some roles are more affected than others by high or low talent. Some jobs are quite repetitive and do not require a great deal of original thought – although it would be dangerous to underestimate opportunities at any level to improve what is done and how it is done. However, any leader will know that they must focus mainly on certain key roles that will make or break a business. In a consultancy this is quite apparent and the 'stars' will be recognisable to almost anyone. In other businesses any leadership or management role has the potential to influence the efficiency or effectiveness of the organisation.

There are a number of theories about how to measure talent. A simple one is to assess everyone according to criteria that you see as important and then grade them into A, B or C categories. The idea is that you can then focus on keeping and nurturing the As, training and developing the Bs, and being ready to replace the Cs as soon as possible.

Malcolm Smith has a slightly different version called FEEL that works on four levels:

Fail = below entry standard, unacceptable performance
Entry = basic performance, competence developing
Excellent = good independent performance, mature competence
Leader = star performance, redefines what is possible, may be a legend in the organisation or industry

Leaders

Malcolm Smith also introduced us to a model for leadership appraisal based on five Es. The best leaders will score highly in each category.

Envision. Constantly seeking better ways to do business. Identifies meaningful and innovative change that produces profitable growth. Comes up with the vision, strategy, and viable plan that will achieve it.

Energy. Excites employees, customers, and partners around winning ideas. Brings extraordinarily high personal energy to everything. Creates an environment where everyone has a passion to excel and an opportunity to contribute.

Edge. Cuts to the essence of what is important. Makes bold, timely decisions. Insists that the organization outperform expectations. Brings a healthy dissatisfaction with the way things are. Makes tough calls when the business or individuals are not performing.

Execute. Focused on results. Avoids blame, seeks solutions. Achieves results significantly better and faster than competitors by employing innovative, proven, and rigorous management practices. Personally meets commitments and keeps promises.

Example. Demonstrates and demands the Right Way. Conducts business ethically. Treats people and all cultures with respect and dignity. Prevents abusive behaviour.

The E-Myth theory

In his book *The E-Myth* Michael E. Gerber describes what happens when most talented people start their own business. They find that life gets much more complicated and, just because they were good at something when working on their own or as an employee, it doesn't mean they can be successful as a business leader. The book is about being an entrepreneur and the theory is that there are three different types of input required for success – talent, management and leadership. Talent is about knowing how to do something well and being able to do it consistently better than others. Management is about developing a process that ensures successful outcomes and being able to pass this on to other people. Leadership is about seeing potential that others cannot and being prepared to take calculated risks to make things happen.

Most of us have some of each of these attributes but have a strong leaning to one of them. The gaps left need to be filled and this can be done by bringing in people who cover the other areas that we do not or learning to cover the gaps ourselves. As most people find it hard to change, the latter course of action is probably the better one in the majority of cases.

Partnering

In my experience, having the right partner makes a huge difference in business. The right partner will be one that brings different skills, knowledge and personality yet shares common ground – usually in terms of values, beliefs and intentions. When partnering works, it is far more effective than one person taking all leadership responsibilities for a business. My own long-standing partner, Bernard Dooling, has a very different personality to me and is much more volatile and excitable whereas I am calmer and more even-tempered. He is much more influenced by what is happening in the moment where I look forward more. What we share is a belief in ourselves and a conviction to be the best we can be and ground-breaking in our work.

Partners can fit and work in many different ways and the job descriptions are often the place to start so that the bases are covered in a practical sense but I believe it is the differences in temperament, not the similarities, that make a partnership strong – as long as there is mutual respect.

The firm as a shared love object

Once people make a commitment to working together, it is important that they give up some of their self-centredness in favour of a positive attitude towards supporting the needs of the firm – much as it is in a positive marriage where each party agrees to give up some of the things they would like as individuals to support the marriage. This creates an enormous difference to the well-being of a business and sense of pulling together. Often the feeling of being part of something bigger is enough reward. However, it may be helpful for the firm to overtly reward behaviours that support the firm.

8.3 Values, Nature and Commonality (Hara)

Values

In chapter six I talked about the values we defined for 20·20. The process of developing these values helped me to understand that there are different types of values and I believe this may help others when identifying and developing their own values. There are three types of values – behaviours, commitments and fundamentals.

Behaviour values are those that everyone can 'see' in that they are the ones that create perception. When we sum up an individual's personality we will describe how they behave – on a day-to-day basis (how we communicate, how we act), under pressure (how we react to stress and conflict) and in times of celebration. The same is true of whole organisations. Behaviour values sum up how people in the organisation are expected to behave and, if they don't, it will be uncomfortable – so much so that people may be asked to leave if they do not or cannot behave in a way that is 'acceptable' within the organisation. Behaviour values will cover things like honesty, openness, dealing with conflict and caring for colleagues and customers.

Commitment values are those that represent a set of intentions. Those values that represent the way we would like things to be and that we will strive for – even though we know we may rarely or never achieve them. Commitment values will cover things like the way we would like teams to operate at their best, the way we expect each individual to be when at work and some description of excellence. The picture we paint when developing our commitment values is the holistic picture we would like to see when we look at our organisation as a whole.

Fundamentals are the values that represent minimum standards at work. This set of values will describe how we expect every member of the team to perform – turning up on time, doing what you say you will do, doing things to the best of your ability, finishing what you start. They are the things you would like to think you don't have to ask because everyone's standards would already dictate that they are done.

Being part of something bigger

All organisations will have values. They may be explicit (expressed and communicated – see below) or implicit (where you find a good or bad reaction to something you do or how you do it). Some organisations go further and include a higher level of belief or community based on a shared awareness – almost a quasi-religious consciousness. This can be based on the Love of the firm (described in the last section) or some other shared belief system. It is not necessary for an organisation to go this far but, if it is there, it can be the most powerful way of harmonising and aligning everyone in the organisation. It is bigger than a set of goals (mainly head-based), it is larger than a familiar and supportive group of people (mainly heart-based) and it is larger than just a set of values (mainly hara-based). Values that are connected to a common purpose can raise the energetics of the business to a higher level.

Sharing your values internally

There are many processes for internal communication and some are more effective than others. As in all communication the principle is to make it a two-way exercise. Broadcasting to a passive audience may get a message across but will never be as powerful as engaging people in it. This can go as far as everyone actively working on the definition of the values or can be working with smaller groups to help integrate the values into the organisation. Taking the values and working on what this would mean in real life is the minimum level of engagement. When working with selected groups, it will be more powerful if the groups are self-selected by asking for volunteers to identify what changes need to take place and then to help make the change happen.

Sharing your values externally

If your business is one where you meet your customers, you cannot fail to share your values – not by communicating them per se but through your behaviours. Ideally the behaviours will reinforce the values you have identified for yourselves. Your employees become the strongest representation of your business or brand values in the way they deal with your customers. In these types of business, it is critical that the management invest time and money in ensuring that all employees know the values and what behaviours are expected of them – as well as checking with customers about how they experience your organisation.

If your business does not deal directly with customers, there will still be some external relationships with other organisations and these will provide some degree of opportunity to express values and receive feedback. However, these may not be enough to create impressions or receive comments on them. Yet there is no doubt that there are plenty of people making comments and these days the comments will not only be shared with a few friends. Social media communities have appeared in the last few years and are now flourishing. A comment made about a company or a brand may be shared with thousands of people within seconds and may generate a huge discussion about the topic shared by millions of people who have never met.

If you care about your business or brand values you will want to know what is being said and have the chance to reply. Being dogmatic or defensive will not help in this virtual community. Being honest is the only way to deal with an event or an issue – and that includes putting right something you are doing wrong.

Internal and external alignment

The most important intention you need to make about this is to align your values and behaviours internally, inside your organisation, and externally, when relating to anyone or any business outside.

Describing a set of values for yourself or your organisation is a complete waste of time if you do not intend to be true to them at all times and in all circumstances. And yet it is surprising how many businesses do not pay attention to this concept – often because they are only using their heads. Adopting the holistic approach to business will ensure that values take their rightful place on the business agenda.

Relationship between corporate values and brand values

Corporate values are holistic and provide the basis for all behaviours and as well as guidance as to what activities a business might become involved in, their attitude to the environment and local community and so on.

Where a business is a brand, the values defined are both corporate values and brand values. Customers will judge the business against its competitors as a brand in the marketplace. The values are intrinsic not ephemeral. They represent real drivers for the lives of the people who work for the business.

Where a business has many brands, the business needs to decide what are shared corporate values and what are specific brand values. A business may have many brands across many markets positioned at different levels in the marketplace – each of which will need to have a different customer perception. At the same time, the umbrella company may well have certain over-riding values that apply to all the brands or possibly values that apply to how it believes they should trade with other companies or how they should deal with employees.

9

GOING LIVE

9.1 The Execution Plan and Goals (Head)

Planning is hard to do well. This is because no-one can suddenly give up the day job to devote time to planning and, at the same time, it is not something that you can just give to someone else to do. The leadership of the business needs to make their own plans and they also need to involve the whole organisation in developing the detailed plans and carrying them out. So, what often happens is that a bit of planning is done and then it peters out as people are 'distracted' by day-to-day issues.

This is not good enough. Unless a business makes new plans it will run out of steam. Remember: "if you always do what you have always done, you will always get what you have always got". And worse than that, if you competitors are making new plans and changes, you will probably find yourself not just standing still but moving backwards relative to the rest of the market. All businesses need refreshing on a regular basis.

So, what is the answer? I believe the way to maintain momentum is to involve the whole organisation in the development and implementation of plans. I do not mean planning by committee but by consensus. This does not entail giving the most junior staff the right to reinvent the business but to involve people at the right moment at the right level. So, the CEO and the board need to lay down the big picture – setting out the ambition, describing the dream and confirming the purpose. The key line managers and specialist managers need to be involved in the definition – developing the proposition, defining the team and confirming the values. It is when 'going live' that the whole organisation needs to get behind the plan and help to make sure it happens.

Objectives, strategies and actions

In classic business planning, you define Objectives, identify Strategies that will achieve the objectives and highlight the Actions that will be required to implement the strategies. This is an iterative process. The headline set of objectives, strategies and actions will lead to a more detailed set. Each set is connected by the Actions from the top level becoming the Objectives of the next level. Here is an example to help illustrate the process:

BOARD LEVEL

O

Objective To broaden our sources of revenue

S

Strategy Increase revenues from sector A

A

Action Develop new product offer(s) for sector A

MANAGEMENT LEVEL

O

Objective To develop new product offer(s) for sector A

S

Strategy Identify market opportunities

A

Action Research customer needs and competitor propositions to identify gaps

Delegate to the experts

Nobody knows the workings of a department better than those in the department. In many cases there will already be lots of ideas of how things could be improved. Some companies ask their employees to come up with ideas on a constant basis but, for those that don't, the planning programme gives a perfect opportunity to do so. Introducing changes that are suggested by the employees is the best way to achieve 'stickiness' – where people are engaged with an idea and work hard to make it happen.

Planning or drowning

Planning has often failed because it has become too unwieldy. It is easy for it to become too burdensome and too detailed – and to become 'too heavy to carry'. The trick is to find the balance between what is needed and what is possible. This is not to say it is ok to give up on planning or saying, "That will do" when you have had enough. It is no good falling short of a good plan and it may be you need to supplement your own time and resources with external assistance – which can have the benefit of not just adding resource but momentum and commitment too. However, you need to judge the organisation's appetite for planning and for change. You need to find that *right* balance – a place where there is sufficient clarity without drowning in detail.

Sometimes this is a matter of editing. If there is too much to handle all at once, you need to prioritise and make sure the most important elements are captured and implemented. Ask yourself, "Where are the big wins?" and also ask, "Where are the quick wins?"

9.2 Team and Roles (Heart)

Roles and people

Once you have worked out your plan you will need to make sure your organisation is in good shape to implement it. Organisation design is a constantly moving feast. It is not a perfect science, more of a 'dark art'. Some businesses can follow the classic prescription of defining the role required and then recruiting a person to fit that role. However, in some organisations, where the people are themselves a key ingredient in the proposition, it may not be so simple. Consultancy is such an example, where the skills, knowledge and even personality of key people can influence the way they are best used.

Building on the E-Myth model

In the last chapter I touched on the E-Myth concept for business leadership. This theory can also be used in organisation design. The *entrepreneur* element is strongly present in any 'market-making' role (marketing, sales, development, etc); the *talent* element is the main ingredient for product and service roles (design, process, product development, etc); the *management* element is the prime requirement for all administration and support roles (office management, project management, IT, etc).

In-house or external?

In the past, most businesses would employ the staff they needed for all roles. In recent years, through the twin pressures of more onerous employment law and economic downturn, many businesses have looked at ways of achieving greater flexibility. This has meant the greater use of freelancers, interims, sub-contractors and consultants. I don't know of any golden rule for deciding when to go outside to fill a role but it is an element well worth taking the trouble to give consideration to when resourcing up for a new plan.

Optimum sizes for business units

There is something special about the size of a business unit. I have long believed that there are two 'break-points' where life changes. The first happens at 30-40 people when a unit becomes too big for true 'informality'. Below that number everyone knows what is happening and what is expected through a kind of osmosis. Everyone is within earshot and the word goes around very quickly. It is very easy to get everyone together for a quick chat or an announcement. Once a group is bigger than about 40, you have to start writing things down and making more formal rules.

The second 'break-point' is at around 100 people. This is where one leader finds it difficult to know everyone personally and starts to lose touch with people. Delegated leadership is necessary and the workforce will feel more detached and remote from the leadership at the centre.

The actual number of people where the 'break-points' happen will depend upon the shape and style of the space in which they work. An open-plan space on one floor will enable a business unit to function longer in the smaller style – so the first break might be at 40-50 people and the second at 120 or so. Groups that interact frequently on shared projects will feel more cohesive than specialist functions that rarely interact.

Managing the size and style of business unit becomes one of the organisational design issues – so a unit that becomes too big can be divided by setting up a subsidiary or a division.

Recruitment

There are plenty of books on the theory of recruitment but I just wanted to touch on it as part of the holistic approach. Recruitment is normally required to fill a specific role, which may have arisen through someone moving on and vacating a position or through a new plan and a change in the organisation design. Having said that, I have found that some of my most successful recruitment has been much more random than that – when someone has been introduced to me or has introduced themselves and I have allowed my intuition to guide me into a decision to take them on. Of course this is easier to do if you are the boss!

The main thing with recruitment is to make sure that the candidate 'fits' your organisation and its values. Skills can be taught but personality cannot change very much. Capability needs to match the job description but it is more important that the person will enhance the organisation through their presence.

9.3 Community Programme (Hara)

Motivations of three levels

Many years ago I saw a play put on by an organisational change consultancy called Vista. I have of course forgotten the detail but the principle has remained with me. There are three levels in any organisation – directors, middle managers and workers – and they have different motivations. The workers get on with their jobs, they are suspicious of everyone else and are primarily interested in survival. The directors are busy looking after their own area of the business and making sure its performance enhances their status and rewards. The middle managers are caught between the two other levels, trying to cope with suspicious workers on the one hand (who used to be their mates) and authoritarian directors on the other (who used to be managers and are so delighted to have moved up to their new level they have quickly forgotten how difficult the middle manager's job was). The middle manager is getting no help from above or below and has the impossible task of getting the workforce to achieve the goals of the directors, which the middle managers were not consulted about in the first place.

This is the natural state for a traditional business organisation, when each level is motivated by self-interest and survival rather the benefit of the organisation as a whole. It is the opposite of alignment and is likely, in the end, to pull the organisation apart at the seams – with each party blaming the others.

Creating community

In the United States in the last 10-15 years there has been a movement towards bringing the whole organisation (or a very large representation of it) together in one place at one time. When done well, this is probably the most effective of all. The general term for this approach is Large Group Interventions and the concept is to 'engage the whole system for rapid change'. Three examples of this are Whole-Scale, Future Search and Open Space Technology.

Whole-Scale. Developed by consultants called Dannemiller Tyson Associates, Whole-Scale works by alternating large group work with small group work. The small groups develop material to bring to the large group and then, after the large group has met, the small groups will take away a series of tasks for further development. The process for a culture or value programme is as follows:

1   Scoping an event planning
2   Leadership team event to define values and behaviours
3   Small group work (data gathering, reviewing, external and internal checking, crafting)
4   Event planning
5   Organisational launch event (whole system involvement in definition and confirmation of values)
6   Small group work (documenting, feedback, plan continuation activities, monitor progress)
7   Event planning
8   Reunion / checkpoint (review commitments, assess progress, learnings, next steps, team organisation)

Whole-Scale can also be used for strategic planning by using their Star of Success, a five-pointed 'route map' that covers the following questions:

1   Do we have the right strategic direction?
2   Do we have the right functions (processes and systems)?
3   Do we have the right form (human, spatial, hierarchical and functional)?
4   Do we have the right resources (capabilities, equipment, finance)?
5   Do we have the right (shared) information?

Each of the questions leads into the next and the whole cycle is iterative.

Future Search. Developed by Marvin Weisbord and Sandra Janoff, but drawing on theory developed by many others, Future Search is designed to explore possible agreements between people with divergent views and is based on seven principles:

1 Get the whole system, or representation of the whole system, in the room at one time.
2 The work that goes on is done in the context of the larger environment.
3 The emphasis is on common ground.
4 Use eight-member groups that are self-managing, directing their own internal process.
5 There are no external experts.
6 It is not a problem-solving conference – problems identified are taken outside.
7 Change involves the whole person: mind, body and spirit.

Open Space Technology. I mentioned Harrison Owen's 'Open Space Technology' earlier as something we had used at 20·20. Unlike Whole-Scale and Future Search, it is not prescriptive in any way. It is the most open-ended process I have ever encountered and, because of this, one of the most powerful – if a little scary at first. Here is a reminder of the rules:

1 Whoever turn up are the right people
2 Whatever happens is the only thing that could happen
3 Whenever it starts is the right time
4 When it's over, it's over

The process takes place in a room where chairs are placed in a circle so that there is no hierarchy and everyone is equal. There is a facilitator but his/her job is to create and maintain a safe place for everyone to feel they can take part. In order to make sure that all voices are heard, an old North American Indian method is used whereby there is a 'talking stick' (or some equivalent) and when someone is holding the talking stick everyone else has to listen and not interrupt.

Without any pre-conceived agenda, an open question is asked – something like, "What do you think needs to change in the organisation to make things better?" When someone stands up and takes the talking stick, it is to state their idea and to commit to helping to make it real. They end by writing their idea on a piece of paper and putting their name against it to confirm their commitment. Then others can decide if they want to take part in helping bring this idea to fruition – and, if they do, they put their name on the same piece of paper alongside the one who first spoke of the idea.

The result is self-generated initiatives and a self-managed system created to implement it. Everyone who has an idea has been heard and everyone is motivated to take forward the ideas that are most supported.

Getting people behind a change programme

What all of these whole system programmes have in common is the idea of motivating people by involving them in the discussions about changes, inviting them to take part in implementing those changes and keeping them updated. Sessions where the whole company gets together at the same time are great but cannot be achieved easily or regularly enough to establish a sufficiently frequent communication. Another way of ensuring people are kept up-to-date is to publish the progress and results on the wall. This may sound a bit like the updates about the church steeple fund but it really does work – particularly if it is updated by the teams responsible for the different initiatives rather than by senior management handing down missives from on high.

Trust • Understanding • Belonging • Incentives

Prof Mark van Vugt's work has provided an interesting four-part guide to creating a successful group based on collaboration.

Institutions that build Trust. This refers to common rules and systems that everyone can see are fair and can buy into. This provides the stability and structure necessary for the group to operate without constantly breaking down and arguing about how things should be done. We are fundamentally tribal and seek groups where we feel we fit in – and our first judgement will be made on the basis of the rules and systems of the group.

Information that builds Understanding. The understanding of our physical and social environment reduces social uncertainty. If you remember your first day at school or at a new job you will know how important this is. It is the lack of information about the new environment that makes us nervous and uncertain. This same drive is reflected when any change happens in the working environment. As soon as changes to the physical environment are introduced (or even talked about) everyone becomes a bit nervous about what it will mean to them. We are territorial and we do not like change – a tricky combination that makes us extremely protective of our status quo.

Identity that builds a sense of Belonging. We need to belong – it is very important for our welfare. A sense of belonging improves and broadens our sense of community. You only have to look at the ever-growing importance of the workplace for our social lives. One third of people now meet their future husband or wife at work. With the breakdown of the family unit, the workplace is becoming more important in providing support.

Incentives that build a sense of Self-enhancement. We need to improve ourselves – if we are not learning new skills we lose our sense of progression. We need to continue to build up our resources and capabilities. If we don't make progress in our current workplace, we will probably look for a new job where we can. For the group to work, the personal incentives and growth opportunities will need to be aligned with the group requirements and benefits.

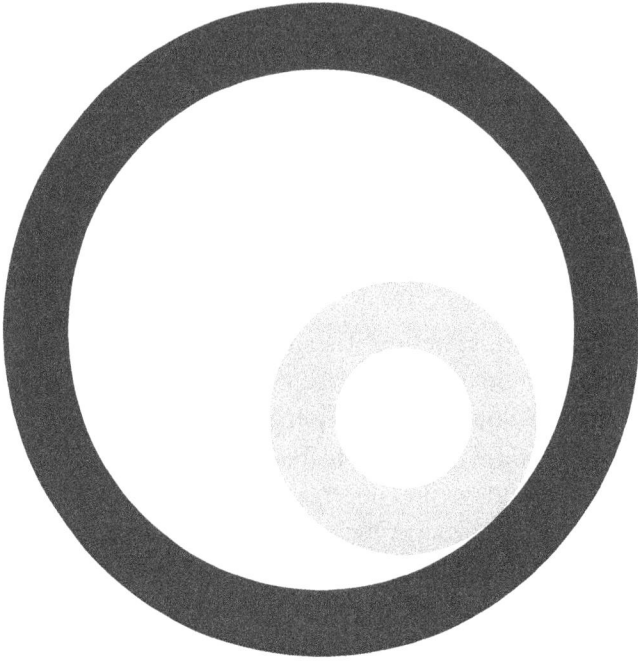

SECTION FOUR
BUSINESS ENERGETICS

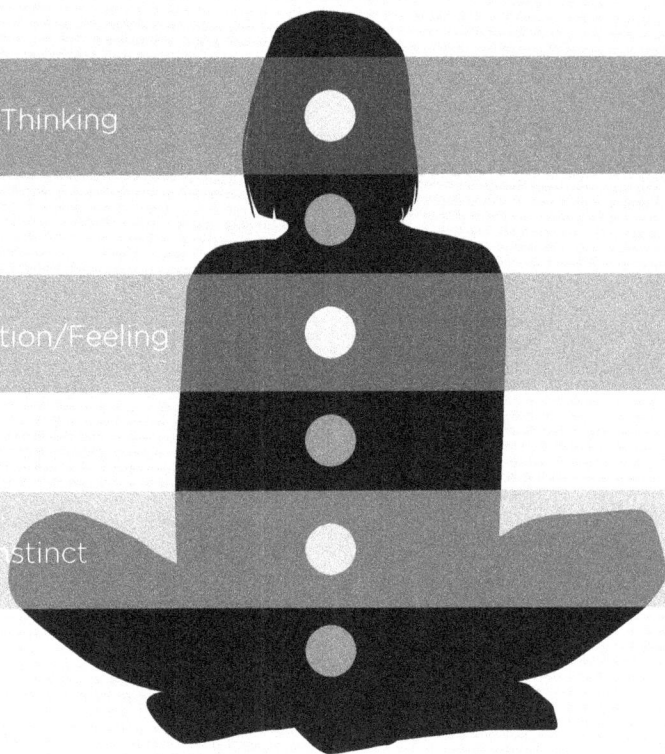

HEAD Mind/Thinking

HEART Emotion/Feeling

HARA Gut/Instinct

10

INTEGRATION AND POSITIVE ENERGY

10.1 Connecting the Three Centres to Higher Elements

If you look again at the Holistic Business model diagram (see below) there is a word at the bottom of each section that describes the energetic quality of each of the business levels – level one = intention; level two = alignment; level three = collaboration. This is where I will outline those concepts.

The Holistic Approach to Business

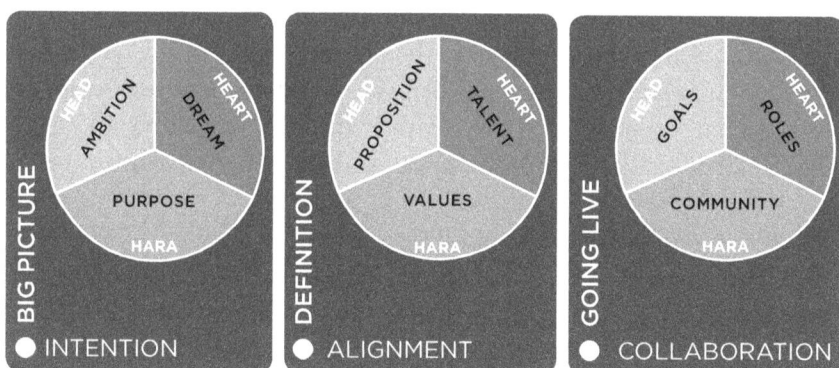

The three centres, head, heart and hara (gut), operate at the material or physical level of life. The concept that elevates the matrix to a higher level is 'energy'. Everything we see and know on this earth is made up of energy, yet we rarely consider this is in our daily lives and even more rarely in our business decisions. It is far too intangible for most people.

However, ask yourself why is it that, with the same knowledge, the same skills and the same experience to tackle the same task, you will perform better on one day than another? What is taking place when an inferior team (in terms of skill) beats the 'better' team? I suggest it has something to do with raised 'energy' levels.

While the world may seem to be physically dense, it is in fact made up of particles that are fundamentally 'energy'. The same is true of each individual human being on this planet. The same is also true of groups of human beings acting together in the form of a business. So, it must be that 'energy' is a key factor in the performance of individuals and groups of human beings.

It can take many forms. Some of these are familiar such as the positive impact of motivational speeches, the power of groups cheering and singing together and the buzz created when a team wins a prize or an award. Some are less familiar. Have you ever been in an office where people are often getting ill? Have you noticed when you move to a new company and feel tired and lethargic, when you would expect to feel energised by the very fact of it being a new job? Do you have a sense of how different you feel when you work in a room with a view of a garden or a park – how much greater the sense of well-being? This is a result of 'subtle energies' that are at work all around us all the time.

Such energetic influence on our lives is often the effect of factors unknown to most of us. Some people are more sensitive than others to subtle energies and may notice such things. Others have studied subjects where such energetic influences are part of the theory – such as homeopathy, kinesiology or energy healing. But you don't have to be an expert or even interested in such subjects to be able to use energy positively in your business.

Intention

Some people see things and say "Why?" but I dream of things that never were and ask "Why not?" George Bernard Shaw

Before someone (maybe you) had the idea of starting the company you work for, there was nothing to belong to or work for. So, every business starts with an idea – an idea that is big enough, exciting enough and well-enough developed to be worth pursuing. First, it has to grab the imagination of the founder(s) and be 'sticky' enough to stay there as an idea all through the difficult process of setting up a business. Then there has to be a clear, strong vision that will attract investors and the first employees. Once a business is well-established, you might think the creation process is all over but you would be wrong. The vision needs to be regularly reviewed and refreshed – what one might call "re-creation". Intriguingly, the word "recreation" means playtime and having fun; this is by no means a bad analogy to use in business as the energetics of developing or evolving the Big Picture can be a lot of fun. If you engage your head, your heart and your intuition in this process, the energy will be powerful and result much more successful.

If you are working with a group of people to do this, try to use stimulus material that will work with these different centres. Words will stimulate the head but images will work better with the heart and movement will help to activate your intuitive nature. Use mind maps to capture your thoughts and discussions as these are more creative than lists and linear records.

Alignment

Not everything that can be counted counts, and not everything that counts can be counted. Albert Einstein

Having a Big Picture is essential but not sufficient to persuade investors or provide direction for employees. The next level, the Definition of the business provides the detailed version, which in turn brings alignment in energetic terms. People who are excited but unclear will be stimulated to act but will not know what it is they are taking part in. They need to know what the game is before they can decide to take part; they will want to know who else is on the team before they join; they will want to know whether they share the values of the team before they can commit to participate and be counted on in good times and bad.

This is clearly true for a new business because there is only a description at this stage and no history. However, it is just as important for an existing business – maybe more so. Why? Because every business or organisation that has history will be riddled with habits and assumptions that will take everyone back to old ways if they are not really clear about the new direction. We are dealing with change and, as discussed earlier, there is huge resistance in all of us to any change.

Again, with this level too, all the centres need to be engaged to trigger the energetic reward. Achieving clarity requires us to describe the 'what', 'where' and 'when' that the head requires; to include the 'who' and 'with what team' that the heart requires; and to express the 'how' and 'guided by what beliefs' that the hara requires. With our heads we can understand an idea, with our hearts we can feel whether it is a good idea and our gut can tell us whether it is the right thing for us and whether we belong.

Collaboration

A tribe including many members who, from possessing in high degree the spirit of patriotism, fidelity, obedience, courage and sympathy, were always ready to aid one another, and to sacrifice themselves for the common good, would be victorious over most other tribes; and this would be natural selection. Charles Darwin

Going Live with a business platform or business model is about operations and day-to-day life at work. We need to know what needs to be done (the plan), what our role is and the roles of others (the team), and how we fit in (the community). Anything less and we will not be able to settle down to our job and do it to the best of our ability.

Energetically, this is about collaboration – the state where people trust each other. They trust that the other person will do the job they are supposed to do; they trust that the team is a good one, made up of talented people and with all the key roles covered; they trust that people will look after each other, will enjoy working together and reap the rewards (which will be fairly distributed).

Trust is hard won and easily lost – and everyone will know when trust is lost. How will you feel if your colleague or your boss asks you to report constantly on what you are doing and how it is going? You will not feel very good. There will usually be one of two reasons for this – the individual's behaviour or the boss' behaviour.

Ask yourself why this might be happening and you will probably find something in the recent past where you have let them down or given them cause for concern. Did you fail to finish a task, fail to do what you promised, say something out of line, turn up late for a meeting or something similar? If this is the case you will have to take responsibility for the loss of trust and work hard to re-establish it.

The other reason for non-trusting behaviour can be fear from 'on high' based on a loss of control. Traditionally bosses were often autocratic and dictatorial, which made them feel good but everyone else feel bad. These days things have changed and employees have much more freedom to decide how and when they will do things (and they feel much more trusted). However, the bosses may well feel a bit out of control in this situation and, every now and then, may push back and act in a more controlling manner (making the employee feel less trusted). In this case the management needs to take responsibility and work hard to re-establish trust.

10.2 My Own Experience

In 2007 my company, 20·20, was faltering. We had a good offer, great history and excellent people – so we thought we had all the head and heart elements covered. And after cuts and changes in 2005 we had a strong year in 2006 and believed we had the hara element right too, with plenty of positive momentum. Yet we hit another bad patch. Although we could have blamed yet another downturn in the economy, I believe most of our problem was to do with being exhausted by the change process of the last three years and some disaffection amongst the top team, where the strain was beginning to tell. For me this was to herald the greatest lesson of all and the strongest proof of the importance of spirit and energetics in business.

At first I could not work out what was wrong but in time I came to see that our problem was the lack of alignment at the top. So I called the top people together, told them what I thought was wrong and asked them if they would be willing to go through a programme to explore and 'fix' the energetics.

Once we had committed to the programme, the four directors met several times for 2-4 hours at a time for a period of 3 months – at first weekly then fortnightly. The first two meetings were run by a psychologist we knew and, more importantly, someone who knew us (he had worked with us a few years ago to help us develop our values). He pushed us quite hard to make sure we all took it seriously and would be really honest with each other. We all had to make a serious decision about whether we were up for the leadership over the next few years and whether we would make a strong commitment to each other and to the firm.

Looking back, I now understand that the stages we had to go through were like dealing with the classic symptoms of grief:

Shock that it had come to this and there was even a doubt that we would all be working together to fix it

Anger that we were in this position

Memories of good times and bad times that we all shared

Despair that we were not all pulling together

Silence and time to contemplate our individual and corporate futures

Questioning how it should be going forward

Vision of how things were going to be and buying in to that future

In the end the whole leadership team stayed in the business but only after some real heart-to-heart honest and robust discussions. We agreed a new vision integrated with a confirmation of our values. This meant that we would:

Be brilliant by being smart and brave

Focus on engagement driven by our commitment to intimacy and impact

Specialise using our focus and passion for people and places where they spend time and money

Do it today here and now – let's get on with it and not be satisfied until we have achieved it

Transformation – a real moment of truth

My original partner and I were still in the business but we all recognised that the business needed to move beyond the founders. The values were pretty much the same but the leaders were changing and the style of leadership was also changing. So, this represented the beginning of a new era. The two founders agreed to step back in a steady and planned way to make room for the two people from the next generation who were ready to take it on.

The next two years were very successful despite a worldwide recession.

10.3 Being Successful

The importance of Being

Most people seem to think that success comes from action, from doing things. Classically management theory would say that it is about doing the right things (strategy and planning) and doing things right (tactical implementation of the plan). While I would support the importance of these two things (after all I have been a strategist most of my life) I believe it is more important to understand the significance of '*being*' than '*doing*'. While involved in personal development programmes I have heard a number of phrases that never seem to come up in business books about the importance of being. Here are some examples.

We are 'human beings' not 'human doings'. We are more than what we do. Learning to BE something rather than just DO something is the ultimate challenge in life. So, why is this ignored in business? Often we do things to keep busy or to avoid the need to think about things. We fill our lives with distractions – TV, books, magazines, the internet, email – that provide a sense of momentum and an assimilation of life but are they really satisfying? It is only when we stop completely that we have the chance to think deeply – or even better stop thinking too and let ourselves be really still. Meditation is a way of putting us in touch with ourselves, calming the constant chatter in the mind and just sitting with the silence and the real beauty of existence.

Your being attracts your life. Do you find that there are periods when things go wrong all the time? If you look closely at how you are during these periods, you will find that you were caught in negative thoughts, depressed, self-centred or some other 'anti-social' state. How do you think people react to you in that state? They are put off having anything to do with you and will avoid your company. On the other hand, when we are 'up' the opposite happens. In an optimistic state we seem to attract nothing but good. People will say, "You are lucky" as though it is all brought about by some external factor called chance. Of course it is nothing of the kind – it is all about your internal state of being.

Be, here, now. The concept of living 'in the now' is an ancient concept for many people but not so much in the Western world and particularly not in the business world. Ram Dass wrote about it in the seventies (*Be Here Now*) and Eckhart Tolle has published several works on the subject (*The Power of Now*) in the last few years and has even appeared on the Oprah Winfrey show bringing the concept to thousands of Americans. The crux of this concept is to be fully engaged in the moment rather than distracted by other things or other thoughts. It is also about living in the present where there is no fear. This is something I considered to be an extraordinary idea when I first heard it but now know it to be wonderfully powerful and releasing. If you think about fear you will realise that it is based only on negative past experiences (your own or someone else's passed on to you in stories) and the projection of these experiences into the future (leading you to fear that a bad experience will be repeated).

With this view of the importance of 'being', I would like to take some time to look at the two words that make up the phrase 'being successful'.

Being = true to yourself

Integrity is terrifically important in business and yet many people in business do not have a clue about what integrity is. Here are a few ideas that may help.

Caring about what you do. "Do what you love and love what you do". When I first heard that sentence I thought it was beautifully simple and at the same time rather clever. Now I realise it is much more that that. It is in fact the most important mantra there is for succeeding in business. Dr Ken Robinson, the inspirational educationalist, talks about people only being able to succeed when they find out what they love to do. He would meet people who were good at something but did not enjoy it – they had pursued one career because someone had encouraged it rather because they had a passion for it.

Sharing the passion with your partners and your employees.
Sustaining a high level of energy in your business is hard to do on your own. So it is critical to have partners and employees that share your passion and help you to maintain the 'fire'. Not everyone has a 'passionate' nature of course but that doesn't matter. People in your business can feel very strongly about things without shouting about it. Recognising and appreciating each person's individual way of expressing their passion or loyalty to the firm is an excellent way of harnessing the positive energy of their personal contribution.

Keeping on course even when battered by storms. Having a strong commitment to common goals will help enormously when things become 'challenging'. Of course it is worrying when things are not going well – sales are down, the bank is being sticky about the overdraft facility, a couple of key people have left to set up on their own. These will be testing times but, handled well, they can provide the very best foundation for the future. The most important thing is to keep your original intentions clear in your mind, remind yourself about what makes you special and do not veer off course.

Successful = achieving your goals

Most people think that success is measured in money. Of course in business you have to make a profit and it is important that you think about making a profit as an extremely positive ambition. In fact the best thing is to involve all employees in the ambition to make profits – and share the profit with them when it is made. However, there are also other ambitions and other measurements of success that are to do with people and posterity.

Financial goals (profit not turnover). Let's look at the profit motive first. "Turnover is for vanity but profits are for sanity". Any observer of the business world will have seen the drive for growth take over the minds of directors who, seemingly caught in the headlights of the oncoming vehicle of their future success, forget to check the most important thing – are we making profits? It seems extraordinary yet it happens a lot. It happened to me in my own company when a new director joined the board and started to talk about growth. We all became excited about the prospect of this dream of a bigger scale and forgot to focus on the bottom line. In four years of growth, our profits went down and down. Somehow there was always a credible reason for this and always a promise that it would "be better next year".

Human goals (helping people to grow). Now this is a really worthwhile goal. "Everyone who works for our company will learn something that will help them grow in stature as a person – not necessarily as an employee." Most businesses only invest in their employees so that they can become more efficient. While this is understandable and would appear to make good business sense, I believe it is a 'limited' view of life that will limit the return on such an investment. A more 'holistic' approach where the whole person is valued as being worth investing in will produce returns such as you could never dream possible. People respond so well to being appreciated and respected for who they are that they will give you far more back than if they think you are investing cynically.

Long-lasting goals (succession). When you start a business your only focus is survival. Eventually you start to believe it will survive (beware this moment as it can lead to complacency) and you even think it might survive beyond your personal leadership. This is a wonderful concept for the founder of any business but it is hard to achieve. The biggest problem is probably you, the founder. To be successful you have probably been a pretty good leader and therefore not that easy to replace. The next biggest problem is finding a suitable replacement. What normally happens is that employees act like employees – not like leaders – because that is what has been expected of them for maybe many years. You could of course bring someone in to take over but this is usually an enormous mistake as they will have no connection with the culture of the business and will therefore often have a negative impact on the energetics of the business.

A Final Word Of Encouragement

Very few things in life that have real value come easily. Maybe the effort we have to put in imbues something with value. Yet, with the effort comes the joy. When we put in the effort to learn a new way or a new skill, the reward can be immense. If the new way brings about a much better outcome, the joy of introducing it into our lives is even greater.

I know the Holistic Business theory will excite some people straight away – they will probably recognise it as something that has been missing in their lives but they couldn't quite put their hand on it. For them, this book will be greeted with open arms (and open hearts) and I am sure it will help them to be more successful. Others will find that it asks a great deal of them and they will be tempted to leave it alone. To them I say, "Let it sit with you for a while and see what comes up." If, in due course, you find that something happens and it reminds you of part of the book, come back and have another look at it – maybe the time will be right for you then if not now.

If you would like to engage with the theory, in order to put into practice, you might think about trying a workshop or two as a way of starting to integrate it into your business.

Whatever you made of the Holistic Business theory, I hope you have taken something positive with you.

Richard

Some of the Sources used

Related Business Books

Arbinger Institute, *Leadership and Self-Deception*
  Berrett-Koehler Publishing; San Francisco, 2000
Baghai, Mehrdad, Stephen Coley and David White
  The Alchemy of Growth, Texere Publishing; London, 1999
Gerber, Michael E., *The E-Myth*
  Harper Business, USA, 1986
Handy, Charles, *The Hungry Spirit*
  Hutchinson Arrow Books; London, 1997
Lorsch, Jay W, and Tierney, Thomas J, *Aligning the Stars*
  Harvard Business School Press; Boston, 2002
Pollard, Dave, *Finding the Sweet Spot*
  Chelsea Green Publishing; Vermont, 2008
Richer, Julian, *The Richer Way*
  Emap Business Communications; London, 1995
Ridderstralle, Jonas, and Nordstrom, Kjell, *Funky Business*
  Book House Publishing; Stockholm, 1999
Semler, Ricardo, *Maverick!*
  Random House; London. 1993

Books About Transformation

Kotter, John, *Leading Change*
  Harvard Business School Press; Boston, 1996
Owen, Harrison, *Open Space Technology: A User's Guide*
  Berrett-Koehler Publishing; San Francisco, 1997
Owen, Harrison, *The Power of Spirit*
  Berrett-Koehler Publishing; San Francisco, 2000
Tyson, Dannemillar, *Whole-Scale Change Toolkit*
  Berrett-Koehler Publishing; San Francisco, 2000
Weisbord, Marvin, and Sandra Janoff, *Future Search*
  Berrett-Koehler Publishing; San Francisco, 1995

Other Books

Covey, Stephen R., *The 7 Habits of Highly Effective People*
  Simon & Schuster; London, 1989
Covey, Stephen R., *The 8th Habit*
  Simon & Schuster; London, 2004
Czikszentmihalyi, Mihaly, *Flow*
  Basic Books; New York, 1997
Csikszentkihalyi, Mihaly, *Good Business*
  Hodder & Stoughton; London, 2003
Gallwey, W. Timothy, *The Inner Game of Tennis*
  Random House; New York, 1974
Goleman, Daniel, *Emotional Intelligence*
  Bloomsbury Publishing; London, 1996
Robinson, Dr Ken, *The Element*
  Allen Lane; London, 2009

Internet sources

Enneagram Institute (www.enneagraminstitute.com)
Ram Dass (www.ramdass.org)
Havard article in September 1996: Building Your Company's Vision
by James C. Collins and Jerry I. Porras (www.hbr.org)
Professor Mark van Vugt (www.professormarkvanvugt.com)
Sir Ken Robinson 2006 TED talk (www.ted.com)
Mihaly Czikszentmihalyi 2004 TED talk (www.ted.com)
Ocean WhiteHawk (www.oceanwhitehawk.com)
The Gyroscope, future shape of the winner – Tom Peters
(www.tompeters.com)

www.ingramcontent.com/pod-product-compliance
Lightning Source LLC
Chambersburg PA
CBHW031418180326
41458CB00002B/427